India – The Peacock's Call

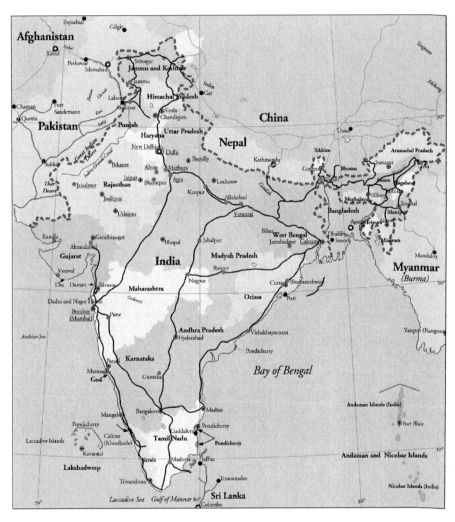

Places underlined are mentioned in the text.

India –
The Peacock's Call

ALINE DOBBIE

SERENDIPITY

First published in 2002 by
Serendipity
Suite 530
37 Store Street
Bloomsbury
London

ISBN 1–84394–010–8

Printed and bound by
Antony Rowe Limited

To contact the author please email:
aline.dobbie@thepeacockscall.com

In memory of my father
Frank Rose

*His deep love and knowledge of India, the
land of my birth, was handed down to me
from infancy – he served India well*

To Richard
with my love
& best wishes

Alwe

Contents

Illustrations

Foreword

by Martin Bell OBE

The Anglo-Indian relationship is a love affair that did not end with divorce. Long after Partition and Independence, it has endured into the twenty-first century. It seems that the British and Indians, bound by the ties of history and language, retain a certain natural affinity. It is not an uncritical relationship: sometimes we exasperate and chide each other, as we might a wayward relative. But there is a mutual fascination always, and never a moment of boredom. It has sometimes seemed to me, in my own travels in India from Simla to Poona and from Bombay to Calcutta, that the Indians are more British than the British. This applies especially to their military culture. If you seek the distillation of Britishness, visit an Indian Army barracks.

Aline Dobbie was born in one, or close by. Her father Colonel Frank Rose, was a British officer in the IXth Jat Regiment of the Indian Army at Bareilly in Uttar Pradesh. He had earned the admiration of his men by leading a daring escape from Singapore as it fell to the Japanese in 1942.

Aline Dobbie left India at the age of 16 and returned 35 years later. *India: The Peacock's Call* is the chronicle of her return. It is more than a travelogue. It is the account of a personal pilgrimage –

not so much a journey abroad but a return home. It is written with grace and affection and a deep understanding of the Indians and their culture. She clearly belongs to the great tradition of indefatigable lady travellers who acquire their history by visiting it: through north central India, from Rajasthan to Uttar Pradesh, one feels that there is hardly a temple or citadel left unvisited. Calcutta and Mumbai (Bombay) are also on the itinerary. Where a hotel's service is less than perfect, which is most rare, or she finds a place she doesn't like (also a rarity – but Bombay is one of them), she is not afraid to say so. Her husband, Graham, on his first visit to India, plays an intriguing walk-on part. What is sometimes alarming to him is reassuring to her. She especially admires the Indians' dignity even in the most adverse circumstances.

Her book serves many purposes, not least to whet the appetite for a passage to India. There are many who will wish to follow her footsteps to some of the lesser-known destinations. *India: The Peacock's Call*, is an excellent travel guide for those who would venture beyond the beaten track. It is also a rare book of discovery.

Martin Bell

Acknowledgements

I should like to thank my husband Graham for his encouragement and love and all my family for their interest and support which pushed me into writing this book. My affection and gratitude for friendship and hospitality in India I hope will be amply demonstrated within the book.

All of the photographs used in this work belong to the author's private collection. The photographs were taken by the author on her visits to India.

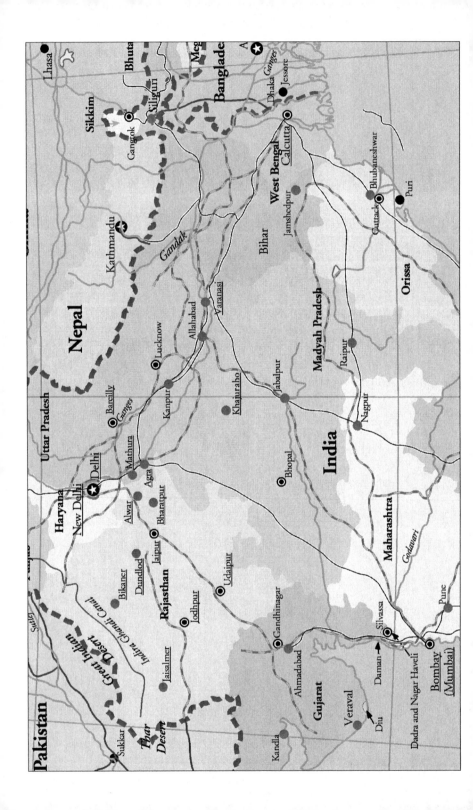

CHAPTER ONE

A Long Anticipated Return

As the great aircraft droned steadily towards its destination I sat back in my seat and thought back to almost 35 years ago. The tarmac at Dum Dum Airport, Calcutta and the tearful farewells to all who mattered in my life apart from my parents. Since a child of ten I had become used to frequent farewells when returning to Britain for schooling, but this was different. This was in effect goodbye to India along with farewell to all who had been so important in my life since I was a baby. As a teenager one is sufficiently realistic to know that this was a whole change in life style and the future though full of hope and challenge would nevertheless be unfamiliar and therefore a little scary. Above all from the 1st April 1963 India would no longer be my beloved 'home'. Now as I watched intently the computer screen of the huge KLM aircraft the red line of the aircraft's path grew closer and closer to Delhi, my destination on this the first return trip all those years later on 1st November. Graham my husband meanwhile was quietly watching me from time to time in between bouts of chuckles; his book was *City of Djinns* by William Dalrymple, a hugely enjoyable read and to my mind almost obligatory if one is going to Delhi. We landed and I found a lump in my throat with the gentle cabin crew greeting of 'Welcome to India' – for me it was of course 'Welcome back'.

Indira Gandhi Airport is the modern Gateway to India and

cannot honestly be said to have any real charm. It should be a showpiece but isn't. First impressions count and it disappointed me that trouble and attention to detail had obviously been spared when this building was constructed; still, having travelled widely in developing countries, it seems that they often cannot appreciate the importance that travellers attach to their first perceptions of a country. As we were later to see, building a good airport is easily within Indian capabilities as Calcutta's internal airport amply demonstrates. The ensuing gentle chaos was extraordinary, not made any better by it being midnight. Four huge aircraft, fully laden, had touched down one after the other disgorging approximately 2,000 people all desperate to extract their respective luggage and depart for their hotels or friends. For us it went on forever and truly ours must have been the very last item of luggage. By the time we emerged and blinked at the battery of people waiting to 'meet and greet' as it is called there was pandemonium. It became obvious that our hostess in Delhi was not there and plan B needed to swing into action. A charming very well dressed young man offered to help me and I gratefully accepted his offer whilst Graham looked after our luggage. He took me to a telephone and thank goodness our hostess Sarup Nehru had just arrived back at her house and was distraught at the idea we were there without her; she had somehow formed the idea we had not arrived on that flight. The portico at the international airport was a complete culture shock to Graham who was looking on bemused as Ambassador after Ambassador car drove up to collect people, horns blaring; hordes descended on some long awaited relative, children raced around, lazy policemen kept a watchful eye, taxi drivers touted for work and other passengers looked as shellshocked as we felt! Our new found acquaintance having helped with the 'phone call promptly summoned a prepaid taxi and we gratefully climbed in, with him giving very explicit instructions to a compliant driver.

The drive into Delhi itself was an experience since neither of us was used to driving in pitch black without any lights on which appeared to be normal practice for most of the vehicles on the road at that hour including our own. It soon became worryingly obvious that our taxi driver was not confident of where he was going and thus it fell to me to use my very rusty Hindi to ascertain directions. The various passers by were amazingly helpful though I suspect not all that accurate, but the *durwans* of the residential colonies did their best. Eventually we realised that the driver was a '*bilkul gomar*' – not bright would be the kindest terminology – and illiterate to boot, thus unable to read the street names be they in Hindi or English. Time was passing and we were increasingly worried, with the driver becoming positively sulky because of course his fare had been prepaid and this was eating into his profit! At last Graham and I worked it out which was no small feat, in the dark in a strange city without the benefit of a street map. Unknown to us the Prime Minister also lived in Western Avenue and when I firmly asked two sleepy policemen in a jeep for directions things began to improve. With relief and joy we finally arrived at Sarup's gate and were warmly received, but by this time the driver could barely speak to us, however my Hindi was coming on in leaps and bounds.

Thankfully after some very welcome tea and a short conversation we went to bed, with the familiar drone of the air-conditioner. The late hour was fortuitous as it proved helpful in that we woke up refreshed in the correct time clock. The sounds of an Indian awakening were immediately familiar. We resolved in future not to use the noisy air-conditioner but the fan instead since the temperature was very pleasant. Maharani Bagh in the morning is full of familiar noises – a man singing happily on his way to work, probably balancing a basket of wares on his head, the *mali* clearing his throat rather ferociously, the purveyor of hot tea and *namkins* shouting his presence to all and sundry, the hooting of the interminable horns, and close at hand the chattering of the Seven Sisters, the green parrots, the crows. I was back and the sounds of my childhood flooded in through the windows whilst I enjoyed a delicious and welcome cup of 'bed tea'. There followed a leap into the shower, some hurried dressing and then an exploration in daylight of Sarup's house and garden. There it all was, the *doob* grass lawn (different to British grass), the bougainvilleas riotous in colour, frangipane (the Temple Tree), oleander, crotons and amazingly the typical chrysanthemums in red terracotta pots. These are the horticultural symbols of winter's approach.

Surendar Singh and Kanti, Sarup's indoor staff, welcomed us and I engaged in some faltering Hindi but it was immediately understood and any mistakes gently corrected. Then ensued a friendly conversation about my roots and family and the fact that Stewart our younger son had been a guest in the home exactly a year earlier. Stewart had backpacked throughout northern India and Nepal for two months the previous autumn and returned home with a journal full of stories and experiences. Now it was our turn. Breakfast was amusing as Graham was plied with rumble tumble (scrambled egg) minus chillies to Surendar Singh's obvious disappointment. Actually Graham became very enthusiastic about the odd bit of chillie in his omelettes as the visit progressed!

Meeting Chotu Nehru again was very special as we worked out that we had not seen each other for over 40 years, our respective schooldays having intervened. We reminisced about happy times as children, the three Nehru boys and me and some of the gentle mischief we engaged in, happy *Diwali* parties, Balo taking us for ice creams to Kwality and the various golden moments of secure childhoods spent in the fifties. There stood Chotu large and handsome and so like his father, who like mine is gone from this world. His mother Sarup is deservedly very proud of him and her two other boys and his extravert friendliness demonstrated to me why he is so successful in his chosen occupation. The rest of the family came in and were all enchanting. We agreed to meet up for dinner that evening but in the meantime our schedule called to us and we departed in the car to our travel agent's office.

Delhi in daylight. Well, yes, it has changed. The capital city of my youth was a superb place of wide vistas and avenues, grand buildings and historic monuments. These are of course still there but not quite so obvious to initial inspection. Delhi has become hugely overpopulated and this becomes distressingly obvious in a short drive. Leaving the leafy confines of Maharani Bagh life is going on all around one, people people and more people, dogs, pigs, cattle, buffalo, goats, hugely impatient traffic, flower sellers, fruit stalls, nut vendors, balloon *wallahs,* cyclists, motor rickshaws, scooters, buses, lorries, the cacophony of sound and visual culture shock is mesmerising. In a very short time one learns not to flinch at a vehicle six inches away from one's shoulder or the hawker shouting his wares through the window – and of course the very poor. Yes, that is arresting to the western eye.

An air-conditioned car created a gentle barrier between the passenger and the spectacle, but on that first drive we were in an ancient Ambassador, hearing, seeing and smelling all of life going on around us. Graham had been prepared for some of what he saw, but nevertheless it is an unforgettable three dimensional experience!

Our travel agent Amit welcomed us warmly and we sat down to finalise our arrangements. His attention to detail and good advice was going to prove immensely helpful. On hearing about the debacle of our arrival he obviously firmly resolved that there would be no such glitches in the future – but this was India and one has, from time to time, to be prepared for unexpected developments. Patience is not a virtue in India, I would say it is an obligatory requirement, but then again a bit of judicious assertiveness works wonders too! A knowledge of Hindi proved situation saving on a number of occasions. We resolved that early next morning Amit would accompany us to the railway station to procure tickets for the Kalka Mail from Varanasi to Calcutta, all efforts to obtain these tickets having failed through the normal channels. Foreign visitors who pay in foreign currency are supplied through a special quota.

Graham and I returned to Sarup's for some very welcome lunch. Our hostess was astounded we did not want to rest, but as we explained, here we were in Delhi with so much to see, rest could come later. I asked the driver to take us to India Gate. In the warm afternoon sunshine there it stood, India's answer to the Arc de Triomphe. For me a daughter of the army, and very proudly the Indian Army, the mother of a serving officer in HM forces, it was a natural act of homage to all those that had given their lives this century for King Emperor and Country and then India Their Country. 85,000 men in the World Wars and North West Frontier, and an eternal flame to those killed in the 1971 war with Pakistan and the Unknown Soldier. When one pays respects, be it in Edinburgh with personal relatives commemorated, or Paris or London; be it on a hillside at Fiesole high above Florence, or the huge graveyards of Athens, this century's cruel marble mementoes along with Normandy and Verdun, one experiences that sad desolation of lives wasted – honourably and courageously given, but nevertheless wasted because of the jealousies, rivalries and greed of mankind. As the Remembrance season approached I thought of our own family's fears for Hamish our big son in Bosnia last year and the fact that he escaped a mortar that fell on the house of his interpreter seconds before he arrived. I thought of India's conflict with China exactly 35 years ago in which I had become involved in a tiny way (helping to organise the evacuation of teaplanters' families from the path of the invading Chinese in Assam). Young *jawans* injured in hospital in Calcutta whom I visited, smelling of gangrene, their lives changed forever because of the injuries suffered. A family steeped in military history is probably the finest grounding for anyone looking back in the closing years of the twentieth century. Civilians sometimes perceive us as a 'gung ho' bunch with an over-eagerness to kill or brutalise. In my experience it is those with a military past who very well understand about commitment, ethos, self discipline and sacrifice, qualities that would be of advantage in all walks of life. The modern soldier moreover has to be a compassionate diplomat as well in our peacekeeping armies. India can proudly claim the world's fourth largest army. As we were to experience in the ensuing few days they have every right to that pride. As befits the world's largest democracy their military forces are professional and first class, but with no thought of usurping the role of democracy.

Walking about in the sunshine Graham was enchanted and interested as was I to observe Indians at leisure. Family groups strolling in the environs of India Gate all resplendent in their

India Gate.

leisure finery, colourful troupes of young ladies, tiny infants, shy little girls, raucous little boys. Much to our amusement there were a group of youngsters splashing naked in one of the formal water channels on either side of India Gate. A good time was being had by all. I espied the familiar snake charmer and he played his instrument to coax the weary cobra to stand erect and spread his hood – what luck, the essence of India. The fruit juice and water sellers urged us to partake but we ever so politely declined! Then on to Rashtrapati Bavan and the Secretariat Buildings. Their very grandeur dwarfs everything. The beauty and magnificence of the two-coloured sandstone dominates but for the scampering of a troupe of monkeys playing on the porticos with the screeching of green parrots as they dart and fly around. On closer inspection there is a little chipmunk who observes one closely from his stone pillared perch. The fact that so many Indians are also promenading and enjoying the sights of their capital made it all the more interesting. Suddenly I would be firmly grasped and pulled politely into a group photograph and then would follow, 'Which your country?' I would answer invariably in Hindi to much delight and further curious questioning. Little girls would sidle up and touch me and dart away when I asked, '*Aap ki naam kya hai?*' A desire to communicate and learn was the overriding impression we gained. Naturally Graham and I were taking photographs and of course there were pleas to include them in the photos – which was a pleasure. A drive round Connaught Place and Jan Path which was looking rather shambolic in the aftermath of *Diwali* and a glance at Graham's face made me instruct the driver, 'Imperial Hotel please for *chaai pani*.' This was a good idea. The old Imperial has been renovated and still retains its charm and ambience. Tea on the terrace is a time honoured tradition. A charming bearer shimmered up and we ordered tea and *gulab jamuns*. Excellent, Graham visibly revived and chortled over his *gulab jamuns*, declaring them to be the very best he had ever tasted. Then ensued a walk through the Aladdin's cave of the hotel shops. How can one refuse to buy with so many enticingly beautiful objects of varying prices to tempt one? Naturally we

Humayun's Tomb, Delhi.

succumbed to the temptation! After this in the twilight we returned home to Western Avenue, very pleased with our first afternoon in Delhi.

Dinner that night was a family affair and immensely enjoyable but not before Kanti had silently appeared with an immensely welcome *taza nimbu* – fresh lime. Oh! that was delightful, and several fresh limes later we enjoyed a superb meal along with three generations of the Nehru family. That was fun and very interesting. Youngsters the world over have the same aspirations and ways of expressing themselves. Sarup talked seriously of India and the family spoke of politics, their family's involvement and about the great and the good of the world whom it had been their privilege to meet. For me hearing recent Indian history from the 'horse's mouth' involving close members of the family tragically now deceased was fascinating. They too were very interested in our opposition political life in South Africa in the seventies. Interest in the British Royal Family is immense in India and I am impressed by the overall affection in which they are held, though with some perceptive observations nevertheless. The year's incredibly tragic events were still a major talking point all over India and particularly in Delhi following so soon on HM's visit and the Commonwealth Heads of Government meeting in our home town of Edinburgh. On the following evening it was again a major topic of conversation at a birthday party given for Chotuji's birthday (wife of Chotu). Having read *The Times of India* on the plane and hearing what various distinguished guests had to say from personal experience of the visit we sadly concluded that the British High Commission and the British Government had badly miscalculated this visit and allowed HM to unwittingly offend quite deeply. None of the anger or outrage was however directed at her personally, except for the bewilderment about the visit to Challianwallah Bagh. 'If you cannot bring yourself to apologise what is the point of the visit . . .?' The current British High Commissioner is not well regarded, and indeed the incredible account of his aggressive questioning of the Indian Prime Minister upon his arrival back in Delhi at the airport invites the question: is he a diplomat? The following evening saw me rigorously questioned about Britain, its new government and the various personalities that comprise the cabinet. Indian social life never flinches from political discussion and I found it all very invigorating, as did Graham. What a refreshing change to reserved Edinburgh dinner parties where nobody wants to be labelled as anything specific and thus insipid conversation about non-controversial subjects lurches on unless one is in the company of very close friends and relatives.

And so to bed after a full day with an even fuller one anticipated tomorrow.

CHAPTER TWO

The Jat Regiment and Bareilly

The crack of dawn found two sleepy Dobbies preparing for a train journey to Bareilly in Uttar Pradesh. Bareilly was and still happily is the Regimental Centre of The Jat Regiment. At the time of my birth they were known as the IX Jat Regiment, meaning they were listed ninth in the British Army listing of Indian Regiments. Today in modern India they are simply The Jats but wisely the IX is retained on their distinctive insignia, though naturally no longer with a crown on the top. Driving through Delhi's early morning commuter/office crush is an interesting experience. Thank goodness for Balvinder Singh's excellent skills! One of the most charming spectacles was the little children all turned out in spotless uniforms patiently waiting with a parent or guardian for their respective school buses. Some of them appeared to emerge from a hole in the wall but nevertheless looked immaculate. I pondered on how those parents coped with all their duties in such disadvantaged conditions. I could stop being prissy and say 'horrible conditions' but then I sound patronising and judgemental – to me they are horrible but to them they are the norm and do not deprive them of their dignity. All over India I was struck by the individual's ability to simply maintain his or her dignity despite some punishing environments. Old Delhi railway station was a special experience, similar to others lodged in my memory but for Graham unique and almost overwhelming.

The coolie who carried our bags was very efficient and took us straight to the Bareilly train where our reservations appeared. We were ready for our adventure!

On time the great train slowly pulled out past the Red Fort, Humayan's Tomb and other notable landmarks. Sadly the glass in the windows was dirty and therefore did not enhance the view, but still it was fun and oh so nostalgic for my umpteen childhood journeys in trains all over India. In those days we had a complete compartment to ourselves and travelled inevitably with all our servants – unless it was for a short holiday in which case only three! The first action my mother would take was to disinfect the lavatory with Dettol! If it was a night journey the berths would be made up and a meal prepared from the picnic ingredients we carried. The fans would be working at full speed to bring some relief from the heat. As an excited child I would have had my face pressed to the window looking out, because even in the dark there was plenty to observe. In the dark hours if one stopped at a major railway station the cacophony of sound continued, with hawkers shouting '*Garam chai*' (hot tea), '*piniko pani*' (drinking water), etc. In the early morning light at a major junction there would be the spectacle of about 5,000 people starting their day with ablutions, exercises, coughing and spitting, selling glorious glass bangles and other exotic wares to the eyes of a small child. At the first real daylight stop my father's manservant would disappear up the platform to the engine and procure hot water for father's shaving, the rest of us would wash in cramped surroundings in the en-suite loo/basin compartment and some form of breakfast would be eaten.

Now in November 1997 my mind wandered back over all these wonderful memories and saw some ghosts, but then that is inevitable. My reverie was interrupted by Graham crowing with delight on spotting an elephant ambling by on a river's edge. There were the same fields, orchards, countryside, all looking very good after the rains, well tended and visibly supporting the often heard declaration that India is now self sufficient in food grains. The little hamlets, the bigger villages looked comfortable; Uttar

Pradesh, India's most populous state appeared to be prosperous. Crossing the Ganges and the Jamuna was for me almost spiritual. Those two rivers had been part of my life for the first sixteen years and I still catch my breath when I see the Ganges. There is something timeless about great rivers in all continents, but for me this time it was a feeling of Land of my Birth, lifeforce, Mother Ganga.

We arrived at Bareilly on time after four and a half hours. After some slight confusion the Brigadier's personal car and driver arrived to collect us. Entering the cantonment in the Brigadier's car is an interesting experience. Everyone who can leaps up and salutes or acknowledges one. Interested eyes take one in, traffic stops. For me however a distant childhood memory was being revived. Long avenues of blue gums; well, here they were, long avenues of blue gums – everything immaculate in the afternoon sunshine at the start of an Indian winter. The Regiment was preparing for Raising Day on 17th and 18th November and everything that could be painted, polished, whitewashed, blue-washed, dug over, replanted or spruced up was having its annual makeover after the rains.

The Jat Regimental Centre was looking sparkling and made me feel so proud. The Jat Regiment was raised in 1795 and celebrated its bicentenary in November 1995. Here again were the buildings so clearly remembered by my mother, depicted in faded black and white photos lovingly preserved by me. In fact we own several good photos of regimental occasions as well as family ones and I had brought them laid out in album pages. These were to prove fascinating to all who saw them and I was beseeched to leave them for the Regimental Museum, but I resisted as they are precious to me. From Brigadiers to Lance Corporal to Mess cook and servant they were intrigued, and of course the same buildings, even the same furniture featured – only the faces had changed. The photos of my parents with me as a tiny baby brought much enjoyment as they now could minutely observe the child grown up fifty years on! We had also put together a short 'brag book' of our family and thus regimental eyes could feast on continuity albeit in another distant land. The warmth of welcome was superb and for me the whole 24 hours was deeply moving and interesting. The hospitality was warm and thoughtful, with a whole suite provided for our comfort. The attention to detail is excellent, but because of the antiquity of some of the buildings and eccentric plumbing etc one could so easily imagine past generals, commanders-in-chiefs and others all staying in these very rooms, set apart from the Officers' Mess for senior guests. On being shown round the mess dining room I pointed out that the chairs appeared to be the same as those in a photo of Daddy with fellow officers taken in 1947.

Jat House has a lovely garden and Brigadier and Mrs Kumar are keen gardeners. Indeed the whole Centre and its environs looked beautiful. Sadly I wished that civilian India would take a leaf out of the Army's book. The Regimental Museum is so interesting and well kept and I presented a bound copy of my late father's story of his escape from Singapore to Ceylon in the company of several others on a flat bottomed Chinese river boat called the Wu Chang. Father also wrote a brief history of The Jats as a people.

Drinks with the Brigadier and his wife were excellent. Mess servants shimmered about with very enticing plates of hot cocktail eats. A visit to the actual mess was interesting to meet old officers and then look at regimental silver and try and identify for what purpose certain pieces were used. Indian messes keep to the same time honoured traditions as we were to experience shortly in Udaipur, but different cultures require different implements, or fewer of them.

Finally we were served dinner in solitary splendour in our private dining room in the guest quarters. It was a fine meal beautifully presented and served with enormous friendship and warmth. Graham quietly observed that he was not used to being watched closely when eating. I explained that was the norm though usually done with discretion. The reason for the blatant curiosity was of course my origin and link with the Regiment. In between mouthfuls I conducted a conversation in Hindi with

Gurung, the very friendly and efficient Lance Naik who was supervising our accommodation. Then in came a second mess servant and finally the cook. They all wanted to shyly converse about the past and what is our present. When we showed appreciation for the cooking the cook promptly went mad and produced fresh *chapattis* one after the other (indeed the very best way to eat them, hot and soft). Gentle questioning followed on our sons, their marriage prospects, what they do. There was evident pleasure that number one son is in the British military, indeed as we spoke acting ADC to the General in Germany. They all agreed that was suitable for a Jat officer's grandson. The fact that his fiancée is also an officer in the army was a bonus. Number two son earned approval for having backpacked in India but why had he not come to Bareilly where they could have looked after him? We were admonished that we must all come again to Bareilly as a total family including 86 year old 'Mummy' so that the Regimental family could look after us. I demurred that Mummy (*mataji*) was now '*bahut purana*' but they declared that an army doctor would be on standby! Indeed the next day I was assured that this would be the case by senior officers. Finally, totally up to the brim with *chapattis* followed by sweetmeats, we said thank you. Gurung wanted to know what we wished for breakfast. I replied papaya, *dulia* porridge (Jat porridge) and eggs.

We retired to our enormous suite of bedroom, dressing room and simple but huge bathroom. Sitting in the bedroom looking at its colonial architecture made me think of the past one hundred and fifty years or so. How many men would have fulfilled their military duties here, reading and writing at the well provided desk? Today there is a modern television with all of India's channels to educate or entertain, but not all that long ago there were only books. In my childhood how many times I had strolled into up-country libraries in district clubs? Books very often partially eaten by white ants, or water stained, most of them without illustrations or eye catching support material, just musty stuffy and sometimes even boring books. Sometimes however there would be a gem and that would keep me from boredom on a long hot afternoon.

Graham constructed the frame for putting on the *machardani* (mosquito net) and we finally slept. I took the precaution of leaving the bathroom light on. There was almost constant electricity but from time to time it could be heard switching over to a military generator presumably when the national grid failed. Visiting the bathroom in the early hours I found myself reacting as of years ago, stopping at the bathroom door to survey the floor carefully (hence the light) so as to avoid any creepy crawlies. These bathrooms have open run-offs for the shower water, and open run-offs provide a welcome for sinister creatures like huge spiders, even scorpions and small snakes. My parents always ensured the outlets were secured with fine mesh to prevent such nasty surprises, but from time to time we had all experienced something unpleasant and potentially dangerous. Mercifully the bathroom was clear but the involuntary act of caution took me back over forty years.

The Indian dawn chorus is both wonderful and raucous. A huge noise really compared to our more melodic one in Britain. Chattering Seven Sisters, cawing crows, twittering parakeets, screeching peacocks, it was all there and in no time at all bed tea arrived with a smiling Gurung. There was too much to see and do and not enough time so we were up promptly. The curtains were drawn for privacy and I was chatting to Graham standing stark naked in the middle of the bedroom. Silly me! I had forgotten I was a guest in an army residence. These messes and suites are not accustomed to female visitors, thus the sergeant in charge of hosting operations had come to discreetly check on his visitors. He was accustomed to casting an eye through a small porthole in the closed door to the adjoining sitting room. He would normally have found a sleepy general or other. He had, I am pretty sure, never before encountered the spectacle of a white nude female, his VIP visitor standing chatting in a relaxed manner in the middle of the bedroom. I suddenly became aware of the silent inspection and darted behind the dressing room door curtains; he attempted to move away discreetly. Graham and I fell about laughing but I knew it would present difficulties later; however we did not meet at breakfast and honour was saved by my careful countenance and complete 'ignorance' when we did.

Stepping out into the sunlit garden in the early sunshine was lovely. Graham and I took some photos which proved to be very successful and captured the morning mist and freshness of the early winter garden. After breakfast the jeep returned with a charming major to accompany us to meet the current residents of my parents' former house, the home to which I had been born. Number 4 Barrack Road has moved a little with the times but in essence is exactly the same. The current colonel and his wife could not have been more charming or welcoming. It was a moving experience for me and not made easy by the interested gaze of a television crew who were there to make a film on the dashing colonel's exploits as a microlite pilot. I reflected that a previous colonel (my late father) had also been a dashing young man, hero to his men at the fall of Singapore, keen shot and the man who brought the Regimental pipe band up to scratch after the end of World War II. Fifty years on here was a close family living in what had been a very happy home for my parents. They were enchanted to see the pictures of it as it was 50 years ago and Graham and I took pictures to show my mother what it looks like today.

After visiting my old home we went to the Brigadier's office to receive an official welcome and meet the senior officers. Brigadier Satish Kumar is a fine man running a superb outfit. There was enormous preparation for the forthcoming Raising day when about twenty-two generals would be descending on the centre for the annual celebrations. It was interesting to see the amount of detail and also the warmth with which old officers of the Jat Regiment were welcomed. India had been independent for fifty years but the bonds between the British officers and the Indian officers and men were strongly present. All around us were the souvenirs of past times with photos of my late guardian Brigadier Bernard Gerty who had taken one of the Japanese surrenders at the end of the war. Having donated a specially bound copy of my late father's articles I was given a beautiful leather wallet and purse with the Jat Regimental crest, and Graham was given a very elegant clock which now sits on his desk.

Having declined to hand over my own treasured photos I had that morning come across the brooch made out of a tiger's collar bone, mounted in gold. This tiger had been shot by my father in the winter of 1950. Today any form of shooting of big game is looked on in abhorrence, understandably, but that tiger had become a serious threat to a local village and was a cattle killer. Father had been asked to come back at Christmas and try and kill it. He had succeeded. In the last days of his life I recall vividly how he regretted killing two tigers and a leopard, but in those days of the 1940s and '50s cattle eaters were routinely despatched. Now India's huge population puts even more pressure on its wildlife and I am resolved to help in my own little way whoever seriously tries to save these wonderful beasts. The tiger collar bone brooch was not something I wore, but I had come across it when packing a few bits of jewellery for the trip. One essential item had been the Jat insignia in silver that had been made into a brooch for me from insignia off father's uniform. Thus when I saw the tiger brooch something made me bring it too! Now here was an opportunity to present it to the Regiment. This gesture was hugely welcomed and immediate efforts were made to type out the caption for the subsequent frame in which it would hang. We were asked for our advice on the accuracy of the English and Graham told them it was called a clavicle.

After the formal welcome Graham and I formally laid a wreath each at The Jat War Memorial. This was beautifully done with soldiers assisting us in full ceremonial dress and the protocol for doing this is outlined in every guest suite so we were well advised and prepared.

Remembrance season for any thoughtful person is a moving time, but here I was within hours of my birthday in the place of my birth laying a wreath. Half a century on it seems we have learnt nothing from all the supreme sacrifice. I thought of the Jat

The JAT Regiment War Memorial at Bareilly.

VCs, the extreme bravery of simple courageous men who helped their comrades in foreign lands. Young Jat soldiers who had never travelled previously suddenly catapulted into the horror of the Second World War, before that the Great War. What must these dignified but simple people have thought about their imperial masters waging war on this huge scale? The Jats are an ancient people with more than one dynasty in eastern Rajasthan and around Bharatpur. Their great ruler was responsible for the victory that resulted in the sack of the Red Fort at Agra and to this day at Deeg some of the spoils of war are still on display outside the beautiful but abandoned palace of Deeg with its eighteenth century gravity fed apparatus to provide spectacular fountains to emulate a monsoon! There are those students of history that think it was entirely possible that the Jats as a race travelled in the distant past as far as northern Europe to the area we now know as Jutland in Denmark. Jats are farmers as well as warriors and the Regiment is justifiably proud of its origins. Now however Indians from diverse backgrounds choose to serve in the Regiment.

I have a cameo memory of one of the superbly turned out ceremonial soldiers holding my handbag whilst I approached and paid homage at the War Memorial escorted formally by his two companions. Major Khulah took us into the Regimental shop and we purchased glasses, ties, swagger stick, insignia. The craft industry worked by soldiers' wives continues to flourish. We met the Regimental Sergeant Major and I conversed with him and thought of the famous Regimental Subadhar Major Hussein Khan who was RSM when I was born. My father was very attached to him and I grew up with a photo of Hussein Khan on father's bookcase. He never spoke English to anyone, though people knew he could converse in English. His logic was that he had learnt English to speak to his King Emperor at the time of the coronation of George VI in 1937 when he represented the Regiment at his coronation – English was only for him and his King! This RSM was as proud and warrior like as all his predecessors and we were glad to meet him.

The major then took us to the hospital where I was born and we met the current doctors and saw that the hospital was flourishing with a sizeable birth rate, far in excess of the number fifty years ago. The last stop before lunch was the Church of St Stephen where I had been christened. This was a simple church built in the early nineteenth century and had undergone the violence of the Indian Mutiny, more tactfully renamed First War of Independence. The priest of the time had been murdered along with a few others and we stopped at their graves in the church garden. St Stephen's is now not an Anglican church but is used under Methodist or Baptist auspices. For years it lay in neglect, and indeed was disused at the time of my birth and my mother had to apply for special permission to use it for my christening – she just particularly liked the look of it. It is heartening to think that Christianity is still vigorous enough in Uttar Pradesh to justify renovating and maintaining it. All over Scotland now small churches are in decline and only used on a part time basis or totally converted to secular use.

It had been a very pleasant morning but filled with emotion as well; Graham and I returned to the suite and changed for our return to Delhi, then we had a delicious lunch. At breakfast I had said we would like *Jat Khana* (Jat food) to the evident delight of Gurung and this was affectionately served. All too soon it was time to leave and everyone lined the steps to say their farewells. Army time is punctual and sadly I was saying thank you to each and every one of them exactly 24 hours after meeting them. Major Khula very perceptively told Gurung to jump into the jeep and we were on our way.

No-one was happy about this railway journey. The Army felt that they should have been allowed to organise it, they worried about the train – it was known to be 24 hours late on some occasions, moreover it originated in what is now a rather lawless part of India and security could be a problem. A box of provisions was thoughtfully provided with a picnic of food, snacks and beer and water to help us endure the journey. We arrived at the station and the major commanded the driver to drive onto the platform – an honour normally only allowed to the Brigadier and Generals. Major Khula said he was going to leave Gurung with us in case we experienced any difficulties, but just as he said this, which we deeply appreciated, the loudspeaker announced the Delhi Bareilly express and the train arrived on time! The major was speechless with surprise; I was privately deeply relieved. We boarded the train with their strict instructions not to mingle with the other passengers. On our outgoing journey we had shyly but firmly started conversations with some of our fellow passengers, but as he pointed out, that train started in Delhi with respectable working people travelling to Moradabad and Bareilly in the course of their work as well as a few families. Now we would be boarding a train that had started 24 hours ago in Bihar and Assam and could have on it all sorts of ruffians and pickpockets. Graham and I resolved to follow his advice faithfully.

The train journey to Delhi was a time of reflection for me. For years I had wanted to make this sentimental journey – almost pilgrimage – to the place of my birth, last seen but hardly remembered in 1950 when I was about three going on four! Now I had been and was gone; I relived all these recent experiences with affection, the people we had met, the atmosphere, the buildings, and wondered sadly if I would ever see it again. Little did I know that within four months I would be back to celebrate the festival of *Holi* with the Regiment. How strange life is: for years my beloved India had been a distant but vivid memory and then quite suddenly the opportunity presents itself for three visits within a space of seven months – truly life has its surprises.

As the evening turned into night and the daylight disappeared we had plenty of opportunity on this dreadfully slow train to observe Indian village life at dusk. Teeming thousands on bicycles, bullock carts, rickshaws, cars, buses, trains, elephants, buffaloes and cattle returning from the fields, herds of goats with minute goatherds and even a few camels though we were in the UP not Rajasthan. The evening fires were lit, people crouched round cooking pots, children were playing in the dust and dirt. That train left Bareilly at about four p.m., late though it had arrived punctually, but it clearly was not going to arrive in Delhi on time! By about 9.30 p.m. it had arrived within a couple of miles of its destination but just sat on a shunting line for over two hours whilst other more important trains hurtled by. That was the dangerous time. Incarcerated in a full train when boredom can set in along with frustration among the rougher elements of the passengers, it was worrying, so finally when the train lurched into Delhi we were very relieved. Our driver was there to greet us on the platform. Thank goodness, the crowds were humungous and moving was a nightmare. Entire families were moving with their bedding and goods and chattels, little girls and boys all holding hands with their shy tired looking mothers. Curiosity is no respecter of time so why not engage in questions! Why was I there, where had I come from to where was I going, how many children did I have, etc. Thankfully we threw ourselves into a clean new *Maruti* car and were whisked away to Maharani Bagh. Arriving at Sarup's we were subjected to a severe scolding on the lateness of the hour, how dinner had been spoiled, what were we thinking of – it took some patience and courtesy to point out that not even we had any influence on the punctuality of the Indian railway system and yes, we were very hungry and exhausted. Sarup said Surinder Singh had even made me a special caramel custard. I gratefully ate it and told him the next day it was a favourite pudding. I reflected that when people have known one since extreme childhood they are inclined to forget the intervening years and make one feel as if a child of four once again!

The next day saw us visiting friends and then having a last lunch with Sarup and discussing all matter of things. How time passes. It would have been good to have a few more days, but hopefully we will see each other again quite soon.

CHAPTER THREE

Land of the Rajputs

The evening saw us winging our way to Udaipur. Ever since I was thirteen I had wanted to visit Udaipur – there was a magic about the place for me with its lakes and palaces. The *Maharana* of Udaipur was to me a title imbued with ancient mystery. Indian Airlines provided a no nonsense service to Udaipur and we were soon installed in our lakeside hotel. The following morning was rewarding. The slap, thud, slap of the rhythm of the women washing clothes on the opposite bank woke me and in no time I was photographing the early morning light. Our room had a balcony right on the water's edge from where one could observe everything. Women singing and washing, birds darting back and forth, the little kingfisher diving down into the lake for fish and returning to the moored boat just beneath me. Before we set off in the car to seriously sight-see we wandered about and took in the far distant views of hills surrounding the lake basin, the brilliance of the bougainvilleas, the oleanders, early poinsettias, morning routines amongst the locals. After the smog of Delhi it was a real pleasure to be in a smaller place with the purity of colour. Udaipur's palaces, palace restaurants, art gallery of miniature paintings, gardens and temples are superb places with so much history and myth. The *Udaipur Rajput* title originates in the 8th century AD and thus has seniority amongst all the *Rajput* titles such as *Jaipur, Jodhpur, Bikaner, Jaisalmer, Kota,* etc.

The Jag Mandir island at sunset. Lake Pichola, Udaipur, Rajasthan.

An ancient land, a fascinating palace, a sparkling day with friendly experiences, what more can one want from a holiday? We were both in our element with the prospect of a fine lunch in a palace restaurant with superb views onto the lake and the various islands of the Lake Palace, Jagmandir, etc. The beauty and tranquillity of Lake Pichola envelop one best in the light of the setting sun; the boat trip to Jag Mandir was so worthwhile. To think that the fabled Shah Jahan as a young prince lived there in exile far outweighs the superficial fantasy of that over-egged James Bond film *Octopussy.*

That evening we were guests of Colonel Gupta and 7 Battalion Jat Regiment. The Colonel sent a jeep with a young lieutenant as an escort. What ensured was pure comedy. Graham and I were formally dressed for an evening function and sitting bolt upright in the back of the jeep. The lieutenant rather shyly and stiffly conversed. The driver who of course was also a soldier was a tall solemn Jat, very serious about his duties. On attempting to leave our lakeside hotel the jeep was surrounded by home-going traffic in the narrow lane. Traffic jams can be desperately frustrating, or simply amusing, this was a mixture of both – but only really for us. Picture if you will a smart white jeep with the large IX Jat insignia, self important Indian officer and driver, two Europeans dressed in smart clothes sitting in the rear, whilst all around is chaos, noisy blaring total chaos, contributed to by immovable holy cows (the driver dare not touch or injure them), pariah dogs, countless men on bicycles, several on scooters, two or three rickshaws and hordes of pedestrians – all it lacked was an elephant or camel! Nobody would give way and everybody with a horn or bell used it ferociously to no avail, including the army driver. It was hilarious for us but we tried so hard to keep straight faces.

The driver was incandescent with frustration and loss of face because he simply was not used to people holding him up. Usually the natural authority of a military vehicle cuts a path through the throng, but this lane was only about 15 feet wide at most, it was Friday night and the end of the week's frustration was evident on all concerned except of course the sundry cows chewing the cud who were really the reason for the chaotic jam initially.

Finally we broke through and were on our way and when we arrived the Colonel and all the other officers and their wives were formally there to greet us. After the introductions the Colonel mildly commented on the longer than usual time it had taken. I could see it was going to be a little embarrassing for the young lieutenant who also did not want to admit that his wrong directions had added to the lateness; meanwhile the driver was standing stiffly to attention in the presence of Colonel Gupta. Fortunately I had the opportunity to turn and thank the driver and tell him his driving was '*bharyia*' (brilliant) – a useful idiomatic expression in modern Hindi. His face lit up and he threw an enthusiastic salute and everyone laughed and lightened the formality.

Drinks on the lawn sitting in a large circle is an age old tradition in India. Mess servants plied us with drinks and delicious hot cocktail eats. Conversation ranged over a broad spectrum and became quite heated at one point, with a young captain taking a verbal swipe at the British imperial past and the modern Royal

Family and the tragic death of Diana, Princess of Wales. Throughout India there appears to be the theory that originated in the Middle East that the princess was murdered. It was a difficult conversation but courtesy ensured they listened to our views. However, Indian dinner parties are vibrant affairs as I have already mentioned and no-one would just be content with trite phrases, nor indeed were we peddling them! Again the photos were of great interest, even here in this Jat mess hundreds of miles away from Bareilly.

Dinner was a very formal meal with thoughtful hospitality and an official photographer. At the end of the meal came the *saunf.* This is based on aniseed and is how an Indian meal concludes with gentle ceremony, rather like an Indian equivalent of passing the port. Each household, mess, restaurant or institution will probably have its own individual mix of *saunf.* Graham and I found 7th Jat's mixture both refreshing and attractive; some can be a little too sweet. Thus Indian mess silver has its own unique vessels or salvers for this ritual. After dinner we took our leave and I thanked them all most sincerely for their warmth of hospitality and said it was quite obvious that as before in my babyhood the old cry '*Jat ki jai*' would hold true. This was well received. Jai is the word for victory, so the Regimental war cry is loosely 'Victory to the Jats!'

CHAPTER FOUR

Ranakpur, Rohet and the Bishnoi

Leaving Udaipur for Ranakpur the next day had its challenges. Another lovely day, my birthday in fact, but I had succumbed to some minor form of stomach bug which can present one with a challenge on a long car journey – and indeed it did, but Balvinder Singh was immediately sympathetic and would pull over in the wink of an eye for me to sort myself out! The only thing to do in the circumstances was to drink Coke and keep off food. The drive was enjoyable otherwise, travelling through the Aravalli hills with their semi desert vegetation. Later I was to see this from the air in daylight and found it really wonderful.

Rajasthan is a dichotomy of ancient grandeur and modern technological wonder. Where else can one sit on a caparisoned elephant talking to someone on a mobile 'phone, or astride a camel as the sun sets and the stars come out and navigate with a satellite compass. More than half of Rajasthan is semi-arid and this desert belt is separated from the rest of the country by the Aravalli Hills, geologically the oldest mountain range in India. People's perception of a desert state before experience does not include shimmering palaces on serene lakes. Intense winter cold is a few weeks later followed by blazing dry heat which we experienced in the summer of 1998 – the record was 49°C. The wide skies of a desert night far from the glow of over burdened cities is clear black and full of twinkling stars, completely silent except for low pitched human conversation and the grunts and chewing of a camel or two. In a period of quiet reflection I thought of this land's ancestry dating beyond 2500BC. It is now generally acknowledged that the Indus Valley civilisation had its origins in north Rajasthan. The Bhil and Milna tribes inhabited this area long before the Aryans thundered onto the scene around 1400BC. The land that the present day Bishnoi are gentle guardians of was once the site of blood and battle interspersed with the gentle teaching of the message of Buddhism in the 2nd and 3rd centuries BC.

Afghans, Turks, Persians, Moghuls followed the Aryan invaders, mixing their blood first in war, then in peace, and thus laying the foundations for the famous martial ancestry of the Rajputs. Whilst in the west in Europe and Britain as we now know them there was a steady decline of the Roman Empire and the fall of Rome to Alaric the Visigoth in AD 410, the Germanic tribes known as Huns, Visigoths, Ostrogoths and Franks were subjecting our northern lands, right down to the Mediterranean countries to barbarism and what was to be known as the dark ages by writers such as Petrarch in the middle ages. Rajasthan from the 7th century to the early 13th century was enjoying a golden age. Thirty-six royal clans who had been successful in persuading the Brahmins of their Hindu faith to provide them with genealogies linking individual dynasties to the sun and the moon developed these competing kingdoms of *Rajputs* (sons of rajas), which led to Rajasthan's original name – Rajputana, Land of the *Rajputs.*

At Ranakpur is the beautiful, pure, clean white Jain temple at which we stopped and rested and enjoyed the beauty of a holy place. Alongside the temple is the *dharamsala* or resting place with cells for visiting pilgrims with its air of peace and tranquillity despite nearby tourist buses and chattering crowds. Ranakpur is set in a peaceful wooded river valley and is a complex of temples founded in the mid-14th century. Chaumukha Temple has a huge walled complex covering 3,600 sq metres on a high stone plinth.

Inside are 29 halls and 1,444 pillars carved from creamy white marble made translucent by the sunshine, each pillar different. Scenes of daily life and images of gods and nymphs and elephants soar into glorious fantasy. The centre is dominated by a huge four-faced idol of Adinath, Giver of Truth. The temple with its total aura of cleanliness thus easily leading one onto thinking purity was immensely restful. Divesting oneself of shoes is no problem for this holy place. A courteous Jain monk will give one gentle background information and then leave one alone to enjoy and absorb the atmosphere. We found it very welcome as by this time my stomach complaint was venting its wrath upon me. Somehow this peaceful cool place gave me strength and we were loath to leave but the schedule beckoned. Near Ranakpur is a charming watering hole called Maharani Bagh where one sits and eats outside under attractive canvas awnings. The choice is varied and the service friendly. Graham enjoyed himself and I asked for papaya from a friendly bearer who immediately took some trouble for me. Fortunately the conveniences are excellent!! Since Balvinder Singh was also now refreshed we were soon on our way after briefly pausing to inspect a rather charming little flock of pink ducks.

The destination was Rohet Garh. This is a charming oasis. The Rohet aristocratic house runs their fort/mansion as a heritage hotel and everything was perfection. Arriving in time for tea on the lawn with the charming family members, guests returning from riding sorties, the sun slowly setting is quite perfect. The buildings are well maintained and more renovations are obviously planned. The gardens are charming with a plethora of bougainvillea, olean-ders, hollyhock, green lawns, a most exotic courtyard pool right outside our suite and peacocks busily walking about. I very soon spied a little man with his assistants painting a mural in the outside dining area beside the pool. His art was charming and though not complete was obviously going to be the beautiful finishing touch to an attractive area. We conversed and he said shyly that he also painted in miniature so naturally I asked to see some of his work. I bought a picture and then a little later saw him again

Sunset at Rohet Garh with peacock roosting.

in a part of the garden where he was obviously allowed to set up his art for the hotel guests. We bought some more paintings as presents for our sons and when I mentioned that this was my birthday he promptly gave me a painting that made a charming pair to the one I had originally purchased. His conversation was gentle and sweet, about his wife, how she also painted (in fact was the artist of the one given to me) etc. Graham and I went up to the roof to watch the setting sun. A tranquil scene of a small lake with island and trees, peacocks settling down to roost, the orange, red glow of the sunset the gentle chatter of birds at the end of the day, waving to little children at their dwelling door, buffaloes and cows returning to their respective byres, what more could one want?

Rohet was filled with French people. This could have been fun as we love France and are well travelled in that country and also understand enough French. It was however tiresome! The French talked loudly and volubly and demanded their drinks orders in French from a patient, shy Rajasthani bearer – speak Hindi, or English and he will leap to serve you but to gesticulate and jabber aggressively in French was stupid. I know the French are very proud of their language but this was taking it to extreme. We watched the charade for a bit and then murmured to the bearer what was required, but the Frenchman simply glared at us and did not even think to say thank you! Their guide was rather supercilious. Graham and I kept our own counsel. Dinner looked perfectly delicious but since I was by now feeling a lot better I did not tempt fate and ate a small amount of rice and lentils.

Siddarth Singh asked us if we would like the following morning to go out into the countryside and visit the villages and see some wildlife. We said that was a lovely idea and after a pleasant night were up very early to see the sun rise. The morning mist gave way to the sun as the temple *pujari* made his morning calls. Standing on the rooftop all was still serene before the bustle of life took over. The horses in their stables, Balvinder Singh cleaning his teeth waving to me in reply to my morning greeting, peacocks starting their raucous morning routine, men coming out of their dwelling for their ablutions on the doorstep, stretching, yawning, praying. We visited the little painter in his room on the way down from the roof. He showed us more of his work and I took a photo of him and his assistants. Perhaps I will send him a copy along with one of all his framed work on our dining room walls. Unsophisticated Indians are always so delighted to be included in a photograph. Some of the painter in residence's work was done on the back of ancient court manuscripts that had been the accounts for the various royal households. Thus the back of the painting is as interesting as the front and one therefore has to take care in framing them; the quality of the paper is unique.

Our host's personal jeep awaited with driver and guide after breakfast by the pool. The French party embarked in two other bigger vehicles and we all set off but our driver did not just follow the others. As we left the confines of the princely fort and navigated our way through the village there was plenty to observe and it was difficult to imagine that it was a Sunday, for nothing seemed to have quietened down – everything that makes up Indian village life was taking place, except the children were not in school uniforms. The drive out into the countryside was pure delight and nostalgic in a way that is difficult to identify. Was it the dryness, the dust, the open plain, vegetation? Certainly the vultures wheeling and resting on a carcase and a feeling of the primitive fundamental aspects of life. Here in the semi desert on the fringes of the Thar Desert which is the most populous desert in the world with some 84 people per square kilometre, life centres around watering holes and grazing areas for flocks of sheep or herds of camels.

The Bishnoi, the most remarkable of desert people, are members of a sect which believes in complete non-violence to all living organisms, and they are the primary reason that desert wildlife still exists in the subcontinent. Bishnoi is an offshoot of Jainism and was founded in 1542 with the fundamental belief that all creatures have a right to life. Just over two centuries ago the Bishnoi defended with their lives their most sacred trees, the Khejri. History recounts that in 1778 the Johdpur administration sent men to cut down these trees to provide firewood needed for burning lime. The villagers defended the trees with their lives and paid the ultimate price with 363 Bishnoi dead. The mass slaughter resulted in a royal decree prohibiting the felling of any tree in a Bishnoi village, and a temple was later constructed at Khejarli in memory of the 363 dead, and every year thousands of Bishnoi arrive to commemorate the sacrifice of their ancestors. The Bishnoi even bury dead chinkara (the Indian gazelle) and erect stones to mark their graves. The Khejri tree is particularly special because its leaves are essential fodder for livestock, its thorns help to protect the desert dwellers from wild animals, its pods are a vital foodstuff and lastly the branches are lopped for firewood. Desert wildlife thrives around a Bishnoi village and a network of natural sanctuaries has resulted from beliefs rooted in the past that hopefully will ensure the survival of many species like the black buck and chinkara in the future.

The jeeps pulled up outside the mud walls of a village and all of us were invited to step inside the village compound. The villagers greeted us shyly and the French with their guide walked

Two brightly dressed young women at the Bishnoi village.

A proud Bishnoi woman who invited me into her spotless village house.

all round gesticulating loudly. It was an outrage in my view they might as well have been in a zoo or safari park. Their manners evaporated and their noisy conversation appeared to us as arrogant and slightly disdainful. This village was as pure an example of Indian pastoral life as it is possible to find. I am not naive or unrealistic about India despite my passion for it, there is a strong possibility that Siddarth Singh of Rohet helps the village headman (the *Sarpanch*) to maintain a perfect tourist attraction – I do not know, but I do know that it was their home, not a National Trust showplace which closes at five o'clock. I asked if might photograph and they said yes, and then a village woman with a superb face invited me into a little house to watch her put on *kajal* round her eyes, whilst her teenage son looked on – all her simple strength and dignity looks out of my photograph. Her kitchen area was spotless and so simple and she made it courteously but firmly clear she did not want me to walk or stand near her hearth.

Graham was interested in the livestock and I talked to the men in Hindi with which they were delighted. The usual questions ensued: was I married, did I have children – two sons met with approval. Then I introduced Graham and they understood and were delighted and talked further and wanted us to photograph them. Looking through a brick archway I saw two beautiful young girls superbly arrayed in Rajasthani village dress, and giggling quietly they posed for a photograph. Pulling water from the village water pump one young mother and child seemed to epitomise simple rural life, and then it was time to move on. We were guests in another village where the highlight was to participate in an opium ceremony. Foolishly in my view some of the tourists actually drank some of the distilled opium. Graham and I wandered away to talk to other villagers. The girls all wanting to know whether my rings were indeed gold. When we departed Graham and I had a quiet chuckle. Our driver considered that as he was driving the ruler's personal jeep he should be allowed to move off first – apart from ego the practical point was that he did not wish to see us covered in a pall of dust. In his indignation he decided to take a different route and that proved very successful for game spotting. We then found ourselves surrounded by a huge flock of sheep and goats, after which came a stately train of camels. All of this was a delight to us and we passed the time of day with the shepherds and camel herdsmen.

Rajasthan does have large flocks of sheep but in the desert where melons and bitter cucumbers sprawl out across the sand for a few short weeks the camel is king. Nearly three-quarters of India's population still lives a traditional life of subsistence farming. Most villagers are poor. They live in simple thatched huts, sleep on rope charpoys or on the floor, fetch water from communal wells and wash in a nearby streams or tanks (man made pool). Few have any education and medical facilities are patchy but most have just enough to eat and life while hard is not impossible. Living close to the land nature is venerated and celebrated in a host of festivals marking the seasons. Driving along a dusty road in Rajasthan, with peacocks in the undergrowth and two or three supremely dignified women arrayed in bright red or orange attire carrying pots on their heads walking along the roadside, is in my mind's eye. I asked Balvinder to slow down sometimes and waved and made a *namaste* sign of respectful greeting to which they responded eagerly with beautiful grins and shy waves. It warmed my heart to see so many small children on weekdays in school uniform and eager to be there. Education is greatly prized in India; would that it were so in our disadvantaged areas of the United Kingdom.

I was to return to Rajasthan in the following March and then again in May just after the Indian nuclear test. The temperature reached a record 49/50°C. The heat was so intense and dry that my face felt crackly and my hair as straw. I thought of the desert people that I had met briefly, those who had no refuge from this intense heat, their simple homes being engulfed by the harsh hot winds called the '*loo*' that is a feature in April and May. In the towns there were booths set up on the roadside for people to be given water as they walked and went about their business. I wondered about the villagers we had spoken with and how they were coping and reflected that perhaps they would be equally appalled by the intense cold we suffer in northern countries.

Certainly there were several fatalities this hot season. Indeed I found myself drinking at least four litres of mineral water daily to maintain a normal body temperature, and that was with the help of fans and air-conditioning.

On our return to Rohet there were the usual sellers of rural fabrics and tourist items. One young girl shyly stood to one side with a cheerful red embroidered throw. It took our fancy and Graham wandered over to bargain – that started a minor scrum but in the end we considered hers was the most attractive and paid the required amount without demur. This was to astonish the sellers and they sweetly pressed us to accept two leather bracelets as well. In the meantime Balvinder Singh had obviously been chatting to all and sundry so several villagers engaged me in conversation and told me who I was – to my surprise. I should not have been, however. In India '*izat*' is important, i.e. prestige, face, what you will. Balvinder had by now decided that he was not chauffeuring just another couple of tourists and that his passengers were worthy of interest. It is one of the endearing things about Indian life, though I suspect the reverse could be very ugly – if you treat people with courtesy but firmness then you receive it back. Friendship and taking an interest in their welfare, buying the third Pepsi, sharing some fruit, allowing time for rest, makes for a hapy journey with a contented driver. In India on those diabolical roads where anything goes that can be a life saving essential!

The dust and dryness were best dealt with by a quick swim and change. All too soon we were leaving Rohet Garh, but I would recommend it to everyone as an oasis of calm and beauty with hospitable host and hostess with plenty of attention to detail. Jodhpur is a short drive away and we arrived at Ajit Bhavan in plenty of time for a light lunch in their enchanting gardens by the side of the pool. We had been allocated a '*rondavel*' suite in the grounds and the hotel was completely full. A thoroughly charming place which is well maintained with courteous staff, Ajit Bhavan had been originally a princely palace which has been well adapted. Jodhpur is a pleasant smallish city with a large military

Swimming Pool at Ajit Bhavan Hotel, Jodhpur.

contingent. The airport is charming and attractive and looking down from the Meherangarh Fort you survey a haze of blue houses; these are the homes of Brahmins, though I believe blue is being widely used now for its obvious attraction.

CHAPTER FIVE

Jodhpur, Osian, Jaisalmer and the Desert

Jodhpur was one of the greatest of the Rajput kingdoms, covering a huge 93,240 sq. km. The royal family claim descent from the great Deccan Rashtrakuta dynasty between the 8th and 10th centuries and through them the sun. On the fall of the Rashtrakuta kingdom they migrated north to Uttar Pradesh, then west. Finally in 1192 Rao Siha moved into the Thar Desert and in 1381 Rao Chunda conquered Mandore. Thus was the desert kingdom of Marwar (Land of Death) and the modern Rathore dynasty born. Centuries ago Jodhpur was a staging post for camel caravans linking China and the Middle East. Today the city has a population of approximately one million but in Indian terms that is small and there are few facilities, though it is the legal capital for Rajasthan. Our guide was a charming articulate young Rajput called Sandeep who gave us an expert tour of the Meherangarh Fort. It is superbly maintained and extremely interesting. The princely cradles and exotic howdahs for ceremonial elephant rides were a highlight for me, whereas the handprints of the various maharanis who committed *sati* or *jauhar* are the most poignant. Some of these courageous women who lived three or four centuries ago fought like men and died by their own hand in self immolation rather than be vanquished by the intruders. What made our whole afternoon so enjoyable was the interesting conversation with Sandeep, who though he speaks excellent English has his Rajput culture visible in his appearance which seems to lie easily with his young modern Indian approach to life. Family life still is of the utmost importance to a man like Sandeep Rathore Singh, and he spoke with pride of his family of five brothers and their wives and aspirations. He is a proud father of a little girl and was dismissive of the boy child cult. The wives however one felt still lived a reclusive life steeped in Rajput convention, quite different from those in the bustling metropolitan cities. Sandeep was a friendly relaxed guide and introduced us to some wonderful shops in the Sardar Market. This market is a must to my mind for any traveller, a true microcosm of India with all of life going on in and around it. Naturally, faced with the enormous range of wonderful goods, Graham and I succumbed and bought. In fact I was to visit Jodhpur a second time and enjoyed it equally then when visiting the famous spice shop and as a guest of Sandeep in his rooftop restaurant with its simple hospitality.

However it is sobering and timely to remember that Phokran is not far from Jodhpur and the site of India's nuclear testing zone. In May immediately after the two nuclear tests, arriving at Jodhpur airport in the extreme heat of midday there was an air of military alertness and readiness that had not been evident when I touched down two months previously in March. No-one should become so enveloped in the faded grandeur of India's past as to dismiss her current military capability. Indians, be they generals, tourist guides or young thrusting Delhi *wallahs* were very defensive of their country's actions and made the point forcibly that India had not in fact instigated either war with Pakistan in 1965 and 1971, nor indeed was she seeking to be warlike now. However the distrust of Pakistan and resentment at the help that country appears to have been given by the USA makes ordinary Indians become quite assertive. It is so sad to hear people in their seventies and upwards reminisce about life in places like Lahore before partition. Even now when Indians go to Lahore on a nostalgic trip more often than not the shopkeepers hark back to the old days and what a beautiful place it was they are only too well aware that Pakistan by most standards is a bankrupt country with little to offer the outsider.

From Jodhpur it is a short drive to Osian. Osian was a major trading centre on the camel caravan routes during the Gupta period (3rd–6th centuries AD). It is now a small market town surrounded by sand dunes. The largest of the Jain temples is dedicated to Mahavira with an idol made of milk and sand covered in 400g of gold and said to be 2,500 years old. We were en route to Jaisalmer and found the whole drive very enjoyable and interesting. The further west you travel into the desert the more dramatic it becomes and I enjoyed it all immensely. Starting after breakfast brings one to Jaisalmer by about 2 p.m. Jaisalmer is a name and a place that caught my fancy way back in the '70s. Apparently Indira Gandhi went there to visit the troops in one of the Indo-Pakistan wars and realised its potential. Until that time it was slowly dying. She realised that the tourist potential of a medieval fortress in its remote desert vastness was enormous and so the roads that had to be built to enable the military to function properly were doubly useful, followed by the Indira Gandhi canal which greatly added to the greening of this desert region and gives its population the essential life force.

As one approaches by car there it is, a magnificent citadel rising from Tricuta Hill like a golden coronet from the desert plain. It is one of the oldest of the Rajasthani forts and was built in 1156 by Prince Jaisal who seized power from his nephew and made it his capital. Legend says the hermit who showed him the spot prophesied that the fort would be sacked two and a half times. Twice in the 14th century the inhabitants committed *jauhar* when faced with retaliatory attacks as a result of their own marauding.

We stayed two nights in Jaisalmer and though we enjoyed ourselves immensely we found our hotel the Shiv Niwas badly run by disagreeable staff. It is a fine building and there was no excuse for poor administration by disagreeable people. The food was quite awful. On our first evening we went to Bada Bagh, the royal cremation ground set between the desert and a rain-fed lake,

Intricate carved detail on exterior of Haveli (mansion) in Jaisalmer.

built by Maharawal Jai Singh II. The memorial *chatris* to the royal dead look superb in the evening light and it is worth it to wait patiently for the sunset. The notice at the Bada Bagh asking people to respect the site and refrain from doing various things is hilarious. The English is so poor that it makes the notice a 'must' to photograph as a modern day contrast to the elegance of centuries past. Sitting chatting gently watching the tourist crowds congregate is always interesting. Most of them simply ignore any requests for respectful behaviour.

The following morning saw us up early and on the flat roof of our hotel to photograph the sunrise and discreetly observe the awakening in the village houses beneath us. Jaisalmer has turquoise as its predominant colour and in these little houses the daily tasks were being undertaken in between washing and feeding livestock. The household goat would stand up and declare he was hungry, all the while behaving like a cockerel standing on a wooden chair in the courtyard; morning fires were being lit, old people came onto the doorstep for their ablutions, the *pujari* rang his temple bells. The *gawalior* (milkseller) would drive his cow from place to place followed by the calf – there was a curious subdued feel to it all. After breakfast we ourselves went with a guide to see the citadel. So much of it is impressive but I found it profoundly disappointing that the filth has been allowed to outweigh its charm. This did not prevent our enjoyment but in such a confined space, though we enjoyed our various meetings with locals such as the busy tailor in his little shop, or the housewife preparing lunch, the stench and effluent became overpowering. Other friends have said they are surprised because a few years ago it was still well maintained. What astounded me continually was the immaculate look of all the business men – their *dhobis* obviously have some magic touch to be able to provide that degree of freshness amongst the squalor.

In contrast the Gadi Sagar was a refreshing delight. Until 1965 it remained the city's only water supply having been built in 1156 and rebuilt in 1367 by Maharawal Garsi Singh. On a sunny November morning standing on the steps at the water's edge it

Gadi Sagar Lake at Jaisalmer.

was a serene spot with the vivid blue of the sky contrasting the golden sandstone. The idea of an all powerful ruler being outmanoeuvred by a prostitute who built the impressive Tilon ki Pol – the palatial archway – was amusing. The story goes that the ruler was so horrified he wanted to tear it down but the astute woman called Tilon speedily built a tiny temple to Krishna on the top of the gate and that ensured the gate's survival.

Jaisalmer has a lot to see in the way of architecture, and the various Havelis are wondrous. We went inside three. One at least is a very attractive shop selling fabrics and *dhurries.* We spent a pleasant hour sipping tea and agonising about which beautiful item to buy and naturally came out with two. So much of the workmanship is superb and the ethnic art coupled with some pieces of antiquity are breathtaking. Every time I walk into our dining room there are happy memories of that morning when I look at the antique sari bedspread sewn in an intricate panelled design, made out of old silver thread sari borders belonging to long gone Indian princesses. We have hung this huge piece from a brass rod on an antique red wall, surrounded by Rajasthani miniature paintings from the different schools of art, i.e. Udaipur, Jodhpur and Jaipur, not forgetting our little friend at Rohet – the painter in residence, who was the only one we actually met. On the floor are two huge *dhurries* bought on a second visit to the famous fabrics shop in the Sardar Market in Jodhpur. Now that is a young wide awake Indian with superb command of English who is a very persuasive salesman, but knowledgeable with it and not too pushy. When it is possible to take the time to sit down, drink tea and also discuss life with these people the whole business becomes such a happy experience. It is really quite easy to communicate through facial expression and body language when one is seriously not interested! I know that the guides invariably get a percentage commission on the sale, but why not; were it not for them we would not know where to go and provided no-one becomes too pushy everyone can be happy. Outright rip-offs do occur, and I feel we were the victims of one such in Delhi, but then no-one pressed us – we simply got carried away with the excitement and ambience.

Lunch that day was a little strange but special and charming. I had read that the Dhola Maru hotel had a good restaurant, so we took the trouble to book a table for lunch and Balvinder duly deposited us there. We were ushered into a strange and enormous basement restaurant and were the only two customers. Graham and I became worried, wondering what was on offer, and since I was only just recovering from a gastric problem a little apprehensive. We need not have been; enthusiastic staff took our vegetarian order and disappeared. One waiter was left to potter around and keep an eye on us. This inevitably led to a conversation in Hindi, which so delighted him that he too rushed off to the confines of the kitchen and eventually the food arrived. It was superb, the delay had been caused by it all being painstakingly freshly cooked – thank goodness – and beautifully presented with enough to feed about six people.

In between mouthfuls the conversation had to continue but they were all delighted at our enjoyment. I am sure at night that restaurant would be a busy place but at lunchtime understandably the tourists were out and about. It proved a cool and friendly haven for us. That afternoon Balvinder and the guide drove us out to Sam Dunes, part of the Desert National Park, to experience a camel ride and see the sunset. Our son Stewart had the previous year spent two days in the desert on a camel safari, but neither Graham nor I could have withstood that. It was not really necessary for me, just riding a camel for a short journey fulfilled my wish. Since a baby I have ridden on elephants, indeed even as a small child gently walked up an elephant's trunk to sit on her shoulders. They are the most intelligent creatures and so affectionate once they recognise one; however, camels have an altogether different reputation and I was slightly apprehensive. The camel owner was a cheeky youngster who was very helpful and friendly; his camel was called Kalu. Graham watched me mount and my obvious delight once up there and then mounted his own beast. The smell was appalling. Camels fart with great vigour and I was downwind of Graham's beast!

We were soon joined by a trio of musicians. All over Rajasthan

Camels awaiting riders at Sam Desert Wildlife Park near Jasalimer.

there are musicians and dancers and after a while one can tire of this, I am sure it is the same for travellers who visit Scotland; the pipes must become quite boring along with all the *tartanalia*. This trio however were fun, they wanted to play, so I said in Hindi it would have to be a short tune as we wanted to get going. This so delighted them that they followed us for quite a distance and eventually we stopped and they sat down in the sand and played a couple of short songs. We applauded and said how much we enjoyed it and took their photo and distributed some money and had the inevitable *limca* drink from a bottle and parted happily. It was fun. Just to have walked out to the edge of the desert would have been like going on a pony ride at the zoo when little, but our little troupe of people and the ensuing conversation made it amusing. Finally we said we had gone far enough and then dismounted and waited for the sun to set, all the while talking and laughing with others, mostly Indian, who were doing the same thing. Our camel owners took us a little apart to enjoy the silence and the beauty. It brought back memories of another desert in another time. As a small child of five I recalled the sunrise on the edge of the desert at Basra, now in Iraq and a very 'no go' area for Europeans! On that occasion the aircraft in which we were returning to India from a home leave was diverted on the orders of the British Prime Minister to collect British personnel working in the oil fields that had been suddenly nationalised. It had been a remarkable journey as the aircraft had touched down in Cairo in the middle of a serious political situation and all of us passengers had been stranded at the airport throughout the day, then allowed into the city by bus, crouching under the seats to avoid sniper fire as we were driven. Hardly had we put our heads down in the old Heliopolis Hotel than we were instructed to get back into the bus and depart for the airport; our BOAC flight had been given permission to depart. As we droned on in this horrid argonaut aircraft the captain of the flight was commanded to divert to Basra and pick up the British evacuees. I was very small but the memory of heat and uncertainty and then the bizarre waiting on the desert's edge by an old Nissan hut for an airport, sitting in wood and rattan chairs in the cold huddled up, just waiting and the sun rising was imprinted on my mind.

Now I was watching the sun set and there was an opportunity to reflect on all that had happened in the intervening forty five years. Memory recall does not actually take very long, but the silence with just a slight breeze stirring and Kalu endlessly chewing and swallowing and regurgitating (as camels do) was impressive. The two Indians had moved away to sit patiently; after all for them this was the equivalent of one of our desk jobs. It was a good experience and then we returned to the tourist car park, but on the way back the camels were frisky, obviously sensing that this was the end of their working day. The young camel owner told me of his young wife and how he planned to expand his business; he asked hopefully for any of my French perfume but I explained that I did not have any on me at the moment! He seemed to accept that readily and was equally pleased with the tip. Driving back to Jaisalmer in the dark with the moon now rising was companionable with the two Indians. We took leave of our guide and thanked Balvinder and said that he should go off and relax as we would find our own way for supper.

We walked through the quiet streets to the roof top restaurant. Walking on Indian streets requires a high degree of vigilance as apart from the traffic the road or pavement can be very messy and full of pot holes and open drains. The shops of course were still open and doing business, but already the little households were obviously settling for the night. Our roof top venue was excellent with a superb view of the floodlit citadel. A party of westerners arrived attired in full Rajasthani dress which we privately thought made them look completely foolish. I suspect that secretly the individuals thought so themselves. Fancy dress is something that is fun when a child, but to see grown hulking Americans decked out in turbans and tunics made it seem rather cheap and demeaning. I thought the world had moved on from the simplistic idea of donning Dutch clogs on a visit to Amsterdam! The food was delicious and as it had taken quite a while to serve us it was late and dark when we carefully descended and wended our way back to our hotel.

We had not brought a torch, but there was some dim street lighting, however we needed to walk carefully in the little lanes. What followed was a charming experience. All the livestock of each household was tethered outside the respective dwellings. Thus you had to walk carefully between contented cows chewing the cud, bulky buffalos, goats with their kids, often bedding themselves down on a piece of outdoor furniture. There was a curious serenity about it. Either there was no electricity to this particular area or the households were very frugal but somehow that quiet walk gave one a glimpse of the heart of India. Yes, this was Jaisalmer, the desert showpiece for tourists, but for these simple people it was their village street at night-time. Just as we had observed them that morning rising and preparing for the day ahead this was the peaceful Indian night and they were recovering from a day's work, as were their respective beasts. Tomorrow their routines would all start again.

CHAPTER SIX

Bikaner, Camels and the Rat Temple

The next morning saw us up early for our drive to Bikaner. Bikaner had been another place that caught my imagination as a child when shown a photograph of the Maharajah of Bikaner who had formed the Camel Corps to help the British in the Great War. He had also been part of the British War Cabinet and finally been witness to the signing of the Armistice in 1918. Eighty years on to look at the photographs of all that generous loyalty to the British Crown makes one think of these splendid figures of history. Some of them had foresight and a sense of responsibility – others sadly seemed completely profligate and the epitome of decadence. The Maharajah of Bikaner was one of Rajasthan and India's bright stars. We arrived after an uneventful drive to stay in the Lalgarh Palace, still home to the present royal family but also a fine hotel. The Bikaner family were established after the foundation of Jodhpur. Jodha Rathore's second son Bika fought with his father, legend has it, or more sensibly realised that a second son would not inherit the throne, and thus headed north deep into the desert. In 1488 he founded his own kingdom of Bikaner. Once again, a hermit prophesied that his dynasty would rule safely for four and a half centuries, and that is what happened since 1947 fulfils the time span. Maharajah Ganga Singh who lived from 1887 to 1943 was probably the most enlightened Rajput of his time. He created roads, railways, schools and hospitals and built the Gang canal which provided irrigation for 290,000 hectares of land. At independence Bikaner became the first Rajput kingdom to join the Indian union. Today it is a thriving city with a medical school, veterinary school, camel breeding farm, and a huge dairy industry which supplies the milk for a large proportion of India's sweetmeats that are manufactured throughout India, not just locally. The local clay is used for the manufacture of sanitary ware, and the hides from the beasts are made into leather. I wish in fact we had been able to spend more time, because not being on the eternal tourist route made it a very pleasant small bustling city.

Our suite of rooms in the royal palace were immense, and photographs showed that at one time they had been used by the current viceroy when visiting. To my mind staying in heritage hotels and establishments makes it all so much more enjoyable; after all, one five or four star hotel in any country is much like another. It would have been nice to see the palace in better condition but from various refurbishments that were taking place that appears to be on the agenda. However, it is always difficult to achieve the perfect touch of maintained history, not over-gilded restoration and country house hotel opulence. After a pleasant lunch we set off to visit the Camel Breeding Farm which had been set up in 1975 by the central government to research their habits and create a superior breeding stock. The Bikaner camel is a more robust, larger beast than the camel seen around Jaisalmer.

Our guide was a charming man with a wealth of knowledge. It transpired that Vijay Singh's father who is still alive had been in the army and been honoured by the building of a roundabout at Jaisalmer to commemorate his heroic feats in the war between India and Pakistan in 1965. It is not normal to commemorate a living hero in this way but he is unique. Vijay Singh was obviously a man of influence in Bikaner with a few interests. His love of family and the ease with which he talked of daily life coupled with his vast historical knowledge made him a good companion.

The camel farm was interesting particularly for Graham who is a vet. We were able to meet one of the vets through Vijay's friendship and have a pleasant discussion. Graham has practised in his own small animal practice, lectured and researched and been a clinician at university and now he manages a large part of an animal charity. So often one meets foreign vets who come to the UK to study or attend conferences, but it is seldom we are able to see them in their own environment. We have a worldwide friendship or acquaintanceship with vets and many of the challenges they face are common throughout the world, but camels are not an everyday beast so proved interesting. It was to be the afternoon of animals, moving from a huge beast of burden to a small creature normally found under the heading 'vermin'!

The Karni Mata Temple at Deshnok is 32 kms south west of Bikaner and our very good friend Monu Basu had said we must visit it. Well, we did, but even Balvinder seemed a bit queasy and admitted he had never been before. Vijay Singh however was full of enthusiasm and explained the legend. Durga, the goddess of war, came down to earth as Karni Mata for 151 years six months and two days. She was renowned as a miracle worker and she married a member of the Charan family – the local rulers. Legend has it that the family members jeered at her powers, refusing to believe in her divinity, so she turned them into rats.

The alternative version is that the family came to her when the young son of one of the brothers died. Karni Mata pleaded with Yama, god of death and the child returned to life; however in exchange all members of the Charan family have to live one life as a rat between human incarnations. Upwards of 20,000 rats at Deshnok are therefore treated with deference and fed by hand on sugar and grain because they are considered honorary humans. As one approaches the temple gates the odd rodent escapes and people lovingly shoo them back or scoop them up and return them. By now I was feeling extremely twitchy as going into the temple required taking off my shoes and walking about in bare feet. Graham's jovial veterinary approach, I noticed, was also leaving him rapidly but he too agreed to do it. Somehow Balvinder managed to enter the confines but hold onto his *chapals*. We however would not have managed that as we were the only Europeans present and thus under close scrutiny.

The whole experience was not too intimidating, but when several rats come and sniff at one's bare feet on the filthy marbled floor it is difficult not to run back. Legend has it that if one is lucky enough to actually see one of the four white rats then good fortune will be round the corner. The place was dirty and literally covered in rats, with people eagerly wanting to touch them and stroke them. Graham thought he would pop his head into the holy of holies and approached the shrine, but just then a rat scampered over his foot and he had visions of it racing up his trouser leg and he beat a rapid retreat. I too was worried though wearing an ankle length skirt. Suddenly Balvinder thumped me on the back, in itself a remarkable gesture, because normally Indian men do not gratuitously touch women, and not in the driver to western passenger relationship. 'Ma'am, come quickly,' he directed, 'I have seen the white rat,' and so I did, almost slipping in heaven knows what. Yes, I did just see the white rat and showed proper pleasure and satisfaction. All around were over the moon. We

The Karni Mata Rat Temple near Bikaner.

duly left and retreated to the car. Graham and I were quite pleased with ourselves and we all chatted happily on the return journey. When we reached our suite I washed my feet vigorously in hot soapy water and sponged out my shoes as well, but no harm befell me or Graham.

We were unadventurous and dined in the hotel which was pleasant though unremarkable. The great red sandstone building had been built in 1902 and encapsulates the royal Rajput slightly heavy look. Edwardian architecture in India, even if built for an Indian, inevitably had a westernised look to it, and quite naturally so if actually designed by a European. Standing in the moonlight on the sandstone terrace or plinth that probably had been designed to accommodate the Maharaja's band or visiting musicians I could almost see the pomp and ceremony of a bygone era – perhaps a visiting viceroy for the shooting, or maybe a member of British royalty doing the grand tour of India; it is not difficult to produce these pictures in my mind's eye because I am fortunate enough to own a very rare copy of *The Face of Mother India*, the sequel to the book *Mother India*, both by Katherine Mayo. This book is so rare that even all our Indian friends pounce on it when given the opportunity. The narrative is factual and traces the history of the subcontinent, but it is the pictures that are archival and superb and capture the whole spirit of empire, dynasties, grandeur, pomp and the mystery and magic of India. The book does not seek to minimise the subcontinent's huge problems of poverty and segregation. To a young reader such as myself all those years ago it was mind boggling. Yes, I was living in India and took much of what went on around for me for granted, but when I read the simple account of the reason and ritual I was appalled. My privileged childhood did not really expose me much to the harsh realities of unforgiving caste and inherent poverty or destitution. My ancestors had served the British Crown through both military and civilian life. Theirs had been a privileged if sometimes difficult time; indeed some had played important parts in the subcontinent's history and been duly recognised. My grandmother Aline de Veria had been a schoolgirl with the girl who was to become famous as the Maharani of Cooch Behar, known to all as 'Ma'. Together they had written and illustrated (my grandmother painted the pictures) a book called *Bengal Decoits and Tigers*. My great grandfather William Rose had as his greatest friend the Maharajah of Patiala and they were neighbours up in Mussorie in the foothills of the Himilayas. Great Grandfather William had at Patiala's request built him a railway for his state, and been rewarded with beautiful mansions built to his specification.

William had also helped Godwin Austin with the Survey of India as a much younger man. My grandfather Geoffrey Rose's eye had been shot accidentally by the Patiala heir when they were young teenagers. Grandfather wore a glass eye which was not even discovered by the army until he suffered a severe bout of dysentery and was hospitalised. On discovery he was honourably discharged from the Army but by this time was a Lt. Colonel, who had served in the Middle East in the First World War. Both Roses, father and son, were engineers, and I thought of how that had leapt two generations to my own sons who are both graduate engineers, one serving in the Army as I write, once more in Bosnia. In Field Marshal Lord Roberts' book *Forty One Years in India* he diarised how the Commander in Chief, General Sir Hugh Rose, treated him with such kindness when serving as his ADC. In time when he himself became Commander in Chief William Rose was Lord Roberts' ADC.

Recently I had the pleasure of listening to a most distinguished Indian lady called Babli Bhagat recalling her early days as an Army officer's wife. Babli also has the rare gift of clear memory and ability to recall defining moments. She lives in Mumbai with her charming husband 'Brig'. They are now senior in years but when they reminisce one is spellbound. Brig's younger brother won the VC at the age of 22 in Eritrea, Brig himself is a brigadier. Babli's early married life when she was only about 20 years of age gave her all sorts of opportunities. She had achieved a double Masters by the age of 20 but wartime India was still a very conservative place and there were only certain types of jobs open to a well born Indian lady. Teaching was one of them but petrol rationing made it impossible for her to take up the position offered and so at the suggestion of her parents who were distinguished in their own right, she joined the military, and was put in the women's arm of the Indian Navy. After six months she was commissioned and stationed in Calcutta. She recollected with clarity receiving the news that her first husband's brother had been killed in the Japanese theatre of war. This recollection was very similar to my own mother Barbara's upon receiving the telegram to say my father was missing. In fact Daddy had made an astonishing escape with his Indian men and helped to sail the Wu Chang all the way to Colombo and resume his wartime career. Babli's brother in law was not in fact dead but a prisoner of war of the Japanese. Babli was sent to London to represent the Indian Navy along with one or two others and this coincided with the end of the war in Europe and she recounted her memories of VE Day in May 1945. Everyone who was there must have unforgettable experiences, and Babli regretted that being so young she did not quite appreciate how historic the day was, but nevertheless she and her little band of friends had some splendid experiences, listening to Churchill, seeing him on the balcony and then later on the balcony of Buckingham Palace with the King and Queen and young princesses. Just finding something pleasant to eat was hard enough but these young women managed with her personality to find themselves tables at notable hotels like the Savoy for a sophisticated but swift meal. The alternative had been spam sandwiches laid on by their Mess. Before departing for India Babli gave her two white silk saris that comprised Indian naval uniform for female officers to a good friend who made them into a very beautiful wedding dress.

Immediate post war India was full of promise for eager educated and well born Indians and for me, a post war baby, it is fascinating to listen to them recalling events leading up to independence and its aftermath. The prophet of Bikaner had said the dynasty would retain power for four and a half centuries. How true were his words. Within the space of a few months was born the world's largest democracy. In the last days of empire new names and faces would become household names, but some things go full circle; my mother told Field Marshal Sir Claude Auchinleck, 'Commander in Chief, you are late, and because of that I have missed the parade I so much wanted to witness – I had to feed my baby ...' The Auk, suitably admonished, apologised profusely and insisted he did not make a habit of being late. That was at Bareilly for the Regimental Reunion of 1947 when several of the soldiers were decorated either posthumously or in person for their courage. I daresay he stayed in the suite of rooms we occupied fifty years later!

Babli recalls those early days of Panditji as Prime Minister. His gentle but firm charm when interviewed by her for a newspaper; yes, he came to breakfast at the instigation of Indira and enjoyed a relaxed family meal and was able to absorb the prime ministerial daily routine, but no, he would not be photographed standing on his head, that was a yoga position to be enjoyed in privacy. She recalls walking out to the car after breakfast and little Rajiv his grandson was holding his hand in the way companionable four year olds do. On being asked by his *Nana* (maternal grandfather) which rose he should put in his buttonhole he would gravely choose one and the *mali* would cut it and fashion it for a buttonhole. Then they would walk to the car with smart attendant driver and guards, and Rajiv would say, 'Nana going or not going?' the little face anxious and hopeful. Sometimes he was rewarded with the trip to the office as a treat by his grandfather.

On reflection I think India was the loser. If Babli had been able to enter politics as she longed to do she would have been a great influence for moderation and integrity, but as she was married at an early age to a potentially very successful army officer who later became General Sen, DSO there was no question of it as politics would have crippled his military career. However her position as a senior army officer's wife gave her opportunities not open to others and she was able to use them constructively and form balanced judgements. Panditji, Indira, Rajiv, Sanjay, these are now the modern legends, and I have no doubt that somewhere there was a prophet who would have prophesied some of the tragedy that enfolded them.

Bikaner's Junagarh Fort is the only fort in Rajasthan that has never been conquered. Built in 1588 it has now been carefully restored and is filled with fabulous furniture and other treasures such as two World War I planes. Oddities abound like the Maharaja's bed which is low on the ground to prevent assassins from hiding beneath and so short the maharajah would presumably sleep with his feet on the ground – in readiness to stand up and fight. Bikaner has a wealth of interest but we were harnessed to a schedule that required us to leave at midday.

As we drove in the heat of the day Balvinder soon suggested we drop into a motel for a short rest and fluid intake. We were only too happy to agree and we stopped and had a cool drink whilst he ate a proper lunch. This odd little rest house was obviously on the side of the road but gave one an opportunity to wander in its grounds and the staff came to talk. It had been opened by Rajiv Gandhi, it transpired, a week before his assassination and his portrait was freshly garlanded in the entrance. The crop around us I was informed was peanut and there were the usual other semi desert crops and an empty swimming pool surrounded by oleanders and bougainvillea. Again there was that peculiar peace one can find even in tumultuous India, with the sound of the busy raucous birds and the bells of some nearby goats. Having met Rajiv on a plane journey when we were both teenagers returning to UK I was still moved by his portrait with its fresh garland of marigolds. There had been a man on whom greatness and destiny had been thrust, he had not wanted it and thus perhaps was not trained to it, and yet honestly, who could be wise enough to take up the reins of:

> the land of dreams and romance, of fabulous wealth and fabulous poverty, of splendour and rags, of palaces and hovels, of famine and pestilence, of djinns and giants ... of tigers and elephants, the cobra and the jungle; the country of a hundred nations and a hundred tongues, of a thousand religions and two million gods, cradle of the human race, mother of history, grandmother of legend great grandmother of tradition ...

and so it goes on, the famous quotation by Mark Twain made in 1897 from *More Tramps Abroad.* The only portion I could remember looking out on the fields was, 'This is indeed India! the land of dreams and romance ...' but I resolved to look it up on my return. A hundred years on those words are as apposite as ever.

CHAPTER SEVEN

Dundlod, and the Shekhavati Region

We were entering the Shekhavati area. The region between Bikaner Jaipur and Alwar was originally a province of Jaipur but it takes its name from Rao Shekhaji who lived in the fifteenth century. He declared independence in 1471 but to this day there are no major cities and it has numerous small forts and palaces and was home to a remarkable group of *marwaris*, who are merchants renowned throughout India for their financial acumen and resulting wealth. I recall some of the famous names in my childhood like Goenkor who were the billionaires of India. They had made vast fortunes in the last two centuries and some of them had spent money on building grand *havelis* in their respective home towns. For the most part these appear to be in disrepair, or run down, but are nevertheless interesting. A skeleton staff inhabits most of the properties and will show you around. There are still some fine frescoes depicting cavalries comprising elephants, horses and camels – martial expeditions appear to have been a favourite subject but since it is all so crumbly and shabby there is not a lot of charm. I wish the wealthy men who own these ancient buildings would spend some of their vast wealth on expert and sympathetic restoration, with an eye to cleaning up the little towns. As in other parts of India the countryside is beautiful but the towns fill one with sadness and some anger. Those who have been fortunate in life and in generational continuity should feel responsibility towards their place of origin.

We continued on the small side roads that eventually led us to Dundlod. This was an intriguing destination. The exterior is like a fort with high strong walls and little of architectural beauty. We drove up to the entrance gate and a servant came out to greet us. We were asked to sign in and then escorted up some old stone stairs to our suite. It was a place of character and charm, evidence of grandeur and history all around us. The bedroom was furnished in an old fashioned style, and the bathroom had the most enormous marble bath that made me think of a tomb. We had requested tea and the cheerful staff member had said, 'Yes, of course.' I heard him talking to someone so I left the room and went on the roof terrace. There was a courtly gentleman who welcomed me and said, 'Ah, you must be Aline Dobbie and you were born in Bareilly!' 'Yes,' I responded, 'but how did you know?' 'Well,' said Thakur Ranbir Singh 'your driver is very proud of you and trumpets your arrival!' A charming story but I suspect the wise old *thakur* quickly makes a bee line for the recent arrival's driver and gives him the third degree, or maybe a cross between the two possibilities.

Staying at Dundlod is a charming respite and one could not want for a more interesting host. Four more guests joined us in due course; they were Swiss and good company. Suddenly the electricity failed which was inevitable but tiresome as it left some of us with wet hair. We all sat in the dark on the terrace and hoped the current would resume in time for dinner. Mercifully it did and we went down into the dining room for the meal. It was good but not memorable. Where there is a hostess the cuisine reaches higher levels. However the Dundlod family were charming when I was to meet them subsequently in Jaipur at their town house. Ranbir Singh's conversation ranged over all the famous princely houses to whom he was related and we were able to have an excellent conversation about people and events over the past 40 years. He is also related to the Patialas and thus was interested in my family's connection there and he pulled out some wonderful old black and white photographs going back to 1911 and the Delhi Durbar. All his uncles had been polo players and some of them had been friends with my late father. Ranbir himself is a playwright and author and considers himself a 'leftie', but he is sufficiently aware of his lineage to be able to recount the past and its glories vividly. The following morning we were up early and in time for the sunrise and the *pujari*'s call to worship. I looked down on the sleepy little town from the fort's high walls and beyond its boundary – there was Balvinder making ready for the day. He always managed to look smart and fresh and I realised how blessed we were to have him as our driver. The previous evening both Swish couples had recounted horrendous stories of their respective drivers' recklessness. Driving is to my mind the only way to see and experience Rajasthan but one does want to reach one's final destination in one piece.

Ranbir told me there were eleven schools now in Dundlod and that was satisfying. Hopefully some of those immensely wealthy *marwaris* channel some of that money into educational and medical improvements if not town planning and renovation. Certainly the aristocracy no longer has the money, nevertheless they possess the dignity. Dundlod is charming but desperately in need of sympathetic refurbishment and indeed maybe that will take place soon as I notice Dundlod features in many advertised itineraries for Indian Grand Tours. We breakfasted on the terrace which was a delight but sadly Graham began to feel really ill (it was a heavy cold probably caught on the flight out), and we resumed our journey to Jaipur, which was not far.

CHAPTER EIGHT

Jaipur on Three Occasions

Jaipur (City of Jai) was built by Maharajah Jai Singh II, ruler of
Amber and a man ahead of his time. Aged eleven years he was
the protégé of Aurangzeb (son of Shah Jehan), a most terrible
man if you consider what he did to most of his close family. Jai
Singh II was responsible for building the new city following the
Hindu principles of perfect architecture with a grid of nine blocks

Amber Palace on the outskirts of Jaipur.

(two occupied by the palace). Main roads were 33m wide and side roads 4m. The local aristocracy and merchants were directed to build courtyard style *havelis,* and the streets were built with colonnades providing shade from the sun to pedestrians. Sadly, these have all been inbuilt now and the charm has faded, but for an early eighteenth-century builder his ideas were superb and the 'old pink city' remains intact. Jai Singh II was building his new city before Edinburgh's New Town was conceived. How I wish the present City of Jaipur would embark on a restoration programme and restore it to the jewel it must have been. When Rajputana became Rajasthan Jaipur became its capital and is now a city of about two million inhabitants.

Having visited Jaipur three times recently I have been fortunate enough to have enjoyed each visit, though none of them was long enough. On each occasion I had the company of an excellent guide who became a friend, Veni Madhaw Sharma. Sharmaji is well educated and knows his history and was a good companion on the first afternoon. Graham retired to bed in the very welcome four star hotel run by Clarks. Being ill in India as a traveller is not funny and a comfortable bed, en suite bathroom and efficient room service and well stocked 'fridge with bottled mineral water is a haven.

I set out in the company of Sharma and Balvinder to see the city. The first stop was Jantar Mantar. This literally means 'instrument to make calculations' and it was built between 1728 and 1734. The Jaipur observatory was the largest and most ambitious of five astronomical observatories constructed by Jai Singh II. He became an astronomer. It has eighteen different instruments used to plot the movement of the sun, stars and moon, and calculate time, date, season, the monsoon and the signs of the zodiac. Sharma showed me the Jantar Mantar in detail and when we checked the time on the hour clock with my battery watch, it was precise and correct to the second! Sharma has to take hundreds of visitors so he asked me to go up the world's largest sundial by myself. I did but decided that coming down was no joke as one can only move sideways to one side holding the wall which pulls

Jantar Mantar.

Jantar Mantar Observatory at Jaipur.

a muscle in one leg descending the steep steps. However the climb had been worth it for the photographic viewpoint of the whole Jantar Mantar and the rear of the Hawa Mahal.

From there we progressed to the City Palace. This was built at the same time as the pink city and is immensely interesting. Probably the most interesting of all the items were the huge silver urns weighing over 340 kgs which were commissioned by Madho Singh II who filled them with Ganges water to take for his visit for the King's coronation in 1902 in London. Jaipur is the city of jewels and so Sharma took me to a huge jewellers where I saw gems the like of which I have never seen before. I was looking for a pair of emeralds and was shown several but in the end they could not find me a perfect baguette cut pair. The price was completely reasonable and in the end I bought garnets which are the local stone for family members. The jeweller agreed to make up a necklace of pearls and garnets in an 'opera' length designed as a gift for my daughter-in-law to be. Her birthday falls at the end of January and garnet is her birthstone. Visiting these jewellers is worthwhile and people should not think they will be exploited.

Provided you know what you want and have some idea of the costs in the West you can make a good bargain. I would stress however that these are large reputable jewellers with sophisticated showrooms mercifully air-conditioned, with cool bottled drinks on hand!

The evening was not a total success. Graham had made a determined effort and showered and changed and I did likewise. The prospect of the Rambagh Palace Hotel was enticing. Built by Ram Singh II, this superb palace was home of the Maharajahs and had its own polo ground. It is superb and sumptuous but not overdone. We had decided to dine and were disappointed that the grandest of the three restaurants was booked out – as it happened fortuitously so!

Graham was still feeling awful but enjoyed a drink in the famous Polo Bar. I lapped it up because the photographs on the walls in this elegant room were all in my memory. Jai the great glamorous polo player was known to me from countless polo games in the 1950s and early '60s. Looking at the pictures and trophies I reflected that it was fitting that he had died from heart disease at the end of a polo match in England. A sad and shocking end for his grieving wife but a wonderful way to go for him! I chose a cocktail which included cream as an ingredient. It seemed delicious, but within minutes I was feeling very odd – since I had decided on non-alcoholic I knew it was not liquor causing me problems. We went into dine and in no time at all I was feeling seriously unwell. Stupidly I ate and then without a word disappeared to the ladies. Doubtless the elegant fellow inmates of the ladies cloakroom thought I was another foolish woman who could not hold her drink. I was too busy to care! When I returned to the restaurant Graham said I was a pale shade of green and we both laughed weakly. What else to do, we had looked forward so much to an evening at The Rambagh, one of the great hotels of the world, only to both feel seriously unwell and incapable of enjoying it. When the resplendent doorman called up our car, Balvinder asked had we had a lovely time, so we replied weakly had he, since he too was dining with a friend and fellow driver.

Oh yes, they replied, an excellent meal. I declined to elaborate on our experiences.

The next day found us both feeling much better and eager to see Amber. Sharma arrived to collect us and we set off for the Fort. It lives up to one's expectations. Built in 1592 the Kuchwaha family reigned here since the 11th century and the surrounding hills are covered in ruins. The ruler Bihar Mal married his daughter Jodhbai to Akbar who built Fatehpur Sikri. Here was a family that not only agreed terms of coexistence with the Moghuls but married into the Moghul dynasty. The waters of Moata Sagar reflect in the bright sunlight the brooding vastness of the fort, and it is fitting that we travel the final few hundred yards by elephant. It was so long since I had ridden an elephant and Graham never had. We had fun and enjoyed ourselves, but I was also sorry to see the great animals so exploited; however, that is India and one should be grateful that the tourist trade enables these elephant owners to make a reasonable living. I have a lovely picture of an elephant in downtown Jaipur, perfectly framed through the car window, juxtapositioned with an ancient cycle rickshaw. Somehow that picture encapsulates India: pedestrians, rickshaw *wallahs*, elephants, car passengers and scooter riders. Sharma gave us a most comprehensive tour of Amber and also treated us to tea in the shade for a rest. On the return journey we paused and looked at Jal Mahal in the centre of the Man Sagar which I notice Ford are using as a backdrop for their advertisements in western newspapers. There is a great deal to see like the Gaitor and Maharani-ki-Chhatri (Kings' and Queens' cenotaphs) and Jaigarh Fort which is another magnificent mountain stronghold dating back to the 11th century but rebuilt by Jai Singh II in 1726.

On a second visit to Jaipur in March I stayed with the Nawab and Begum of Loharu at Loharu House. They run their city mansion as a charming Pay and Stay establishment. The welcome is very personal and the attention and service could not be improved. I personally greatly valued my conversation with the Loharu couple and revelled in their household of attentive friendly

Jaipur's ancient means of transport.

servants and the feeling of family that took me back to my own childhood; excellent food with little details like homemade jams and chutneys from the garden produce. The garden is large and well maintained with an orchard area and back garden. Loharu is a small place north of Jaipur, technically in Haryana, but like Dundlod and Mandawa. The Nawab is a parliamentarian and at the time of my visit thinking deeply on the new Indian Government and its widely publicised religious beliefs and trumpeted intolerance of other religions. We both hoped that it was part of the rhetoric of general elections and that their more pragmatic personalities would have a benign influence. The Nawab was very well travelled and over the years had met many world famous people who were all captured in photographs positioned round the drawing room. We did not in fact sit in this room, preferring the veranda, but it was irresistible as a photo subject with its great stuffed tiger standing in the centre. On this occasion I had driven from Jodhpur to Jaipur and resolved firmly never to do such a dangerous thing again. That particular stretch of road is part of the main Delhi to Mumbai highway and a constant stream of heavy overladen lorries travel night and day at breakneck speed, with total disregard for other road users. We were pushed off the road on three occasions and had our car's driver's side mirror ripped off. All along the road there are wrecks and obvious signs of fatalities. On this occasion we did not have the trusty Balvinder and were the poorer for his absence. Indian drivers are very good if one considers the driving conditions and over population, but some are either lacking in imagination or anxious to reach a further incarnation.

On my third visit to Jaipur on business in May we stayed at the Rajputana Sheraton and were very thankful for its air-conditioning and elegant facilities. The Welcome Group who own the various Sheraton hotels such as the Maurya in Delhi and others in all the major cities have a special place in my heart as the company is part of the great ITC Group, one of the huge conglomerates that bestride the Indian industrial and commercial scene. Indeed one of our greatest friends Monu Basu had been its managing director, but in my teenage years he had been a junior executive to my late father. This was the start of a great friendship and to this day both Monu and Champak Basu are inclined to remind me that they have known me since a child of twelve if they think I am getting above myself. I in turn recollect that their very talented daughter Srila, who is India's only glass blowing artist, used to leap into my lap as a tiny child in 1962 and demand to know how many babies I had and who was my 'uncle', i.e. husband. I would say no babies and no husband – which was a relief all round considering I was only fifteen, but Srila would leap off in disgust and my standing in her eyes was ruined!

The heat of May was truly stunning and I would not recommend that time of year for purely tourist activities, however there were many from Spain and France and I wondered how they could endure the heat in the various tourist attractions and outside. We had flown into Jaipur on this occasion and the day had reached a record temperature which made the aircraft's landing particularly difficult for the lady pilot with all the thermal currents. I had again been saddened as it was the anniversary of Rajiv Gandhi's death and all the papers were full of commemorative photographs and here we were on an Indian Airlines aircraft, which in his vital days as a young man he had probably captained himself. Jaipur like Jodhpur has a good airport and is well maintained. My strong recommendation to travellers would be to arrive by air or rail, or perhaps from the north by car, but on no account from Jodhpur by road. In the extreme heat the importance of colour seemed to strike me more forcibly. Colour has great significance in traditional Rajasthani dress. Only Rajput men can wear yellow turbans, those who are Brahmins can wear orange and yellow, while businessmen wear orange, lower castes dark red, and farmers and those in mourning, white. The younger women wear saris or embroidered skirts and bodices of pink, red, yellow and orange; those in black, blue, green, grey or white are widows.

On this last occasion we were able to visit Anokhi and see some of the wonderful hand printed clothes, soft furnishings and accessories. They now have shops in many countries but Jaipur was the original and the shop is a delight. Now in two of my bedrooms the bright and cheerful colours of Rajasthan are reminders of a happy time. Lovers of blue and white would find it particularly worthwhile.

The last two days in Jaipur in May were enjoyable as we were able to relax a little and were treated to some excellent and friendly hospitality by the manager of the Rajputana Sheraton, George Verghese. George originates in Kerala and extolled its virtues to us. Indeed I already knew because Hamish our eldest son and his wife Vicky went there for their honeymoon at the end of '97 and had a glorious time. They had rented a villa close to Kovalam beach and also visited Cochin, and experienced a backwaters journey on a houseboat, with glorious food and a gentle mode of transport. They had managed to fit in a visit to Periyar and ride elephants and help to bathe them, and their photographs are truly beautiful. George did not have to persuade us too much that Kerala should be our next destination in India. Indeed Babli Bhagat urged us to fly out to stay with them in Mumbai and then all of us should go down to Kerala to a friend's house – yes, that indeed would be special. Being a houseguest in India is so relaxing. Indians are famous for their hospitality and justifiably so. Nothing gives me greater pleasure than to be enfolded in the heart of a large Indian family and enjoy their spirited conversations and leisure pursuits, golf being high on their agenda.

This essence of family I had further experienced in Bareilly in March. Had someone said to me that after 35 years I would be back in Bareilly twice in five months I would have laughed, but so it was. We were able to share their *Holi* festivities. The traditional Hindu festival of colour celebrates the end of winter, the destruction of the demon Holika and the veneration of Kama, god of love, and his wife Rati, goddess of passion. People mark the day by bombarding each other with coloured water, dye, or in poorer villages watery clay and cattle dung and by drinking marijuana-based *bhang*. In various cities there are also accompanying festivals like in Jaipur which has its Elephant Festival. However as a guest of the Commandant of The Jat Regimental Centre we played a rather dignified version of *Holi*, with, I am glad to say, pure colour powder with no adulterations that might be harmful.

We arrived at 8.00 a.m. having left Delhi on a nightmare drive at 4.00 a.m., to avoid roadside revellers. Even in the darkness one could see people lighting the spring fire and winding themselves up for further merriment. Our journey suddenly became very dangerous because we drove into a pea soup fog and the driver and I decided to proceed with extreme caution as there was nowhere on the roadside where we could stop safely, no-one else thought of stopping and the idea of a huge lorry driving into the back of us was appalling. However we suddenly drove out of the fog into the sunrise and Bareilly on *Holi* day awaited us.

Satish and Saroj Kumar were still in their night clothes but welcomed us warmly and the telephone started ringing with everyone calling to wish 'Happy *Holi*' rather as we would say 'Happy Christmas'. The Jat House staff were happy to see me again and plied us with sweetmeats and sweet tea. We were shown to our suite and chose the one adjacent to the previously used set of rooms. Gurung, who was in excellent form, arranged some fruit for breakfast and then we changed for the *Holi* party. The officers and their families all came in old and shabby clothes, but we had not brought our gardening togs and anyway I suspect it would not have met with approval had I arrived in some faded dungarees! We were driven to Jat House and the moment we arrived the young officers who recognised me from my previous visit covered us in bright yellow and red and orange powder. The obvious affection and friendship was heart warming and I loved it all. To be in Bareilly, my birthplace, on a clear beautiful spring day with the Jat House garden ablaze with flowers, friendly people hugging one and smearing one's face and hair, well, that is an unique experience and one of my most treasured memories. Food was laid out as a buffet and we gorged ourselves on further *namkins* and sweetmeats. Gurung was the most attentive of stewards, and how I wished Graham could have been there along with our two sons. This was a regimental family in the Indian Army enjoying itself on one of its special days. Tiny tots ran around and were scooped up and plastered with yellow powder, the Brigadier was having a wonderful time as were the young men, then Colonel Vijay Singh arrived and I was so pleased to see him and meet his wife who was so gentle and murmured that she was fasting for the day. Having been a guest in British Army messes with our son Hamish it was lovely to experience the present buzz and exuberance of their counterparts in the Indian Army.

Lunch was to be at the Officers' Mess and I cleaned up a bit for that. The officers and their families were going to play Housy Housy and we joined in, it was amusing. Finally lunch was served

Aline Dobbie covered in colour playing Holi with Jat Regiment officers.

Brigadier Satish and his wife, Saroj.

Army Officers' Children.

and I was invited to help myself to food along with the Brigadier's wife. There was a glorious array and silence gradually reigned whilst we all ate with enthusiasm. Brigadier Satish and his wife then said they would leave and that was the signal that we would all disband. A welcome shower was in order and a scrub of the clothes I had worn – mercifully the cleaning agent with which I always travel now made short work of the garments, but curiously it took much longer to rid oneself of the colour in the hair and skin, though by the next day it had completely disappeared without any allergic reaction.

Sitting on the veranda outside our suite I saw Gurung cycle by off duty now and ready to play *Holi* with his fellow soldiers. Shyly they would come and chat to me whilst I wrote a letter home. These young soldiers and their older brothers in arms are fine people, with an eagerness to learn and communicate. This time I had brought them the colour photos of Hamish and Vicky's wedding and they were delighted with that as it showed the ceremonial uniforms of the British Army and all the colour and tradition of a big wedding. In between the chat was that peculiar silence again, interspersed by the call of the peacock on the wall, some chattering monkeys and the noisy Seven Sisters birds. I was weary after my pre-dawn departure and the stress of the car journey, but I did not want to sleep and miss any of the experiences on offer. Fortunately the photographs of that happy day have developed beautifully and will always be a memento.

CHAPTER NINE

Chandra Mahal, Deeg & Bharatpur

When we said farewell to Sharmaji that first time in November we left for Chandra Mahal Haveli at Pehersar, just within the boundaries of Rajasthan, very close to Bharatpur and Deeg. This is a Jat area and the Jat farmers constitute a small percentage of the population and are chiefly concentrated in areas close to Delhi and Haryana. Rajasthan had two Jat kingdoms, Bharatpur and Dolpur, but it is believed by some that the Shekhawati region was also held by the Jats. Our host at Chandra Mahal is a Jat with an illustrious father who in his young days had been Commandant of the Governor General's Bodyguard to Lord Mountbatten. He is married to a beautiful woman from the Jodhpur royal house and together they run a superb establishment in their ancestral home. Young Amit, our travel arranger, had wisely thought to book us in here, and we were so pleased with the arrangement. Munna and Giri Singh are charming and the house is beautifully but simply appointed and one is invited to feel as a personal guest. The cooking is a celebration and the rooms are simple and attractive. The architecture of the mansion cum fort is very heavy on the exterior but true to the *haveli* tradition there is an inner courtyard off which there are verandas and suites of rooms, with narrow little stairs taking one to the flat rooftop from which there is an excellent view into the village surroundings. The gardens are a picture, and since I was lucky enough to be a luncheon guest in March as well I know that they provide a colourful haven throughout the tourist months. Indeed Giri's hollyhocks were to be envied and when we remarked upon them in November she immediately directed her *mali* to provide me with some seeds. I thought that a few in an envelope would be forthcoming, but in fact I came back with a full plastic bag and today there are hollyhocks from Rajasthan growing in Peeblesshire.

That first evening I ran up to the roof to see the setting sun and try to photograph it, but in fact I had to be patient until the sunrise because the light had gone very quickly. In the morning light it was enchanting watching yet again Indian village life at the start of the day, with the little children waving and calling greetings. The buffaloes were coming out of their byres and a village woman was busy sculpting cow pats into cakes to dry on the roof to make fuel for her family. A peacock was busy pecking at a pumpkin plant that was growing nearby on the roof and the road sweeper was making a faint effort to clean up the main mud thoroughfare.

We left Chandra Mahal to visit the Keoladeo Ghana Bird Sanctuary at Bharatpur. Today it is world famous for its bird life but before independence its fame was more generic. Bharatpur was the premier Jat state and is a legacy of Churaman, a Jat overlord whose forces were a source of constant irritation to the Moghuls in the late 17th century. The Moghuls retaliated by destroying the Jat villages but they later regrouped under a leader called Baden Singh who firmly entrenched himself in the region beside the Jamuna river between Agra and Delhi. Baden Singh built the fort and palace of Deeg in 1725. A short time later his son laid the foundation nearby of the fort at Bharatpur. Bharatpur's fort was never taken by the British though they laid siege to it several times. The fort was made impregnable through the simple device of surrounding it with massive earth walls and a moat. Today Bharatpur has little charm in my view but is a must to visit for the bird sanctuary. Deeg however is a showcase of Jat architecture and has several trophies of war including a marble swing that belonged to Shah Jehan and was taken by Maharaja Suraj Mal in his successful sack of both Delhi and Agra forts.

Upon arrival at the bird sanctuary a large problem emerged. We had sufficient funds in travellers' cheques and credit cards but we appeared to be very low in Indian currency. There was a small entry fee to pay and then the rickshaw *wallah* to pay and it is not a good idea to be without small change in India at any time. Balvinder sweetly offered us some money and a young rickshaw *wallah* came up and asked us to use his services. We said yes but that we had this problem with a cash shortage. Devi Singh was his name and he confidently said that it would be no problem and we should go with him. It is lovely once one enters the park as only authorised vehicles are allowed and everyone else has to use a cycle or a cycle rickshaw. The atmosphere was peaceful and relaxing and already the heat of the day was increasing. Devi Singh first of all took us to the Forest Lodge Hotel to exchange our travellers' cheques, but it was Sunday and they would not do so under any circumstances as we were not residents. So Graham and I thought, well, we must simply register as hotel guests and pay for a day's tariff. No, said the clerk, he could not offer us a room as he was fully booked. Interestingly there was almost no-one around. We replied that we did not need accommodation but would be happy to register and pay the tariff and thus be allowed to cash our cheques. He said that could not be done and would look odd in his book-keeping so we had to come away defeated and a little worried. Devi Singh said not to worry, he would find some British tourists and maybe we could exchange some sterling. Fortunately I had £20 in my purse. The first cycle tourist turned out to be an American who though sympathetic could not help, and then along came a pair of British who understood our dilemma and were happy to exchange a ten pound note for Indian rupees. Thank goodness, neither of us knew how we had allowed this situation to develop but it could have put a blight on the day until we arrived at our hotel in the evening.

Devi Singh was very knowledgeable about the bird life and we began to enjoy it. On another occasion we hope to spend a couple of days and rise very early and watch the birds on the marsh as well as in the trees. The sanctuary has 360 species of bird and among the bulbuls, doves, egrets and ducks are seven species of birds of prey, several species of heron, stork and owl and a migrant population of rare Siberian cranes. There are also animals including chittal, sambar, nilgai, blackbuck, jungle cats and python. In 1733 the Maharaja dammed several small rivers to create marshland breeding grounds for ducks. These would provide sport for the famous Bharatpur duck shoots for people like the Viceroy when they came as guests. 250 years later it became a national park.

The conversation with Devi Singh ranged over life and his aspirations as a family man, that he needed a greater income than what was on offer from being a rickshaw *wallah* – after all that is very seasonal – and when we left him we took his address and have kept in touch. I later met Devi Singh again in Agra in March when he came to my hotel to meet me. Sometimes India is so frustrating for the Westerner. The Devi Singhs of India are hard working simple people who would dearly love to have second and third incomes, but it needs someone to find the opportunity for them and bureaucratic India can make that very difficult by obfuscation and delay.

At the gates of the park there are the usual fruit sellers and we were tempted by the papaya (*paw paw*) vendor. He had some huge papayas and now we had the cash with which to buy a couple. Graham and I tried always to have a fresh papaya in the car because it provides a moist and delicious snack which is hygienic provided one does not put any of the skin in one's mouth; moreover should one have an irritable stomach papaya will actually help to soothe and cure the malady.

Deeg is a short drive from Bharatpur and well worth the detour. The actual citadel was built in 1730 and dismantled by the British in 1804 and now only the 28 metre high wall remains. In 1768 the Maharajah built himself a stunning summer palace of yellow stone. The central building, the Gopal Bhawan, is flanked on either side by barge-shaped pavilions. In front are laid out large gardens, which today are not very well maintained and at the rear is a huge green tank (man made lake) which is the water supply for the locals. That Maharajah had an obsession with water. The gardens and the buildings on the water's edge are filled with nearly 2,000 fountains all designed to create an artificial monsoon. The Keshav Bhawan pavilion used jets of water to roll stone balls and recreate the sound of thunder and for the Maharajah's birthday the fountains' pipes would be filled with dye and the fountains flowed in rainbow colours. Sadly, nowadays these water extravaganzas only take place for three days in the year. We were the only Europeans present and the resident guide caretaker came forward and invited us in and took us round the palace, which is extraordinary in that it has been left as it was with stuffed tigers, elephant's foot furniture, sofas, chairs, pianos, beds and other memorabilia. The atmosphere is not eerie but odd as if one has walked into a faded palatial stage set. We both enjoyed the experience and when it came to saying thank you I realised that once again we were short of cash, having paid Devi Singh, the money owed to Balvinder and the papaya seller! So I proffered a tip and explained in Hindi what had happened. The caretaker was so kind and said no, *memsahib* must not be without money and he would not dream of taking anything and leaving us in a difficulty! However I pressed it on him saying his excellent guidance could not go unrewarded and we parted friends. Much to my annoyance the film in the camera at this point, unknown to me, had not wound on properly so I have only one photograph of Deeg and none of Kaleodeo Bird Sanctuary. From Deeg we had to retrace our drive to Bharatpur and Balvinder said we should stop for a rest. He chose an awful place which confirmed my worst nightmare about Indian style lavatories.

In fact when well maintained these are extremely hygienic and not at all a problem provided one wears a longish skirt. Trousers for obvious reasons could be a big problem, and especially if there are some evil looking fluids swilling around. It is curious that a race that tries whenever possible to take a great interest in personal hygiene and appearance should have so little interest in lavatories.

After all, that is a place we all have to visit, and indeed the five-star hotels and other institutions have marble floors and gleaming sanitary ware with gold plated taps and attendants. Middle of the road hostelries have less attractive facilities of both western and eastern design and the rest are just simply awful, including those on the train. When I emerged out of this example Balvinder looked very sheepish and apologised and I brushed it off to save him embarrassment, but then men do not most of the time have quite the same requirements!

We very soon reached Agra, and on the way saw the outlines of the fabled Fatehpur Sikri. We had to press on however because Taj (as it is called) is closed on a Monday and therefore we needed to visit on the Sunday afternoon and then again at sunrise on the Tuesday morning. On the Monday we planned to visit the Red fort at Agra and anything else and then drive back the short journey to Fatehpur Sikri. The plan worked superbly and we went straight to the Taj Mahal on arrival in Agra. It was a beautiful afternoon, bright and clear and cool.

CHAPTER TEN

Agra and the Sublime Taj Mahal

'O Soul, thou are at rest. Return to the Lord, at peace with
Him and He at peace with you. So enter as one of His
servants. And enter into His garden.'

The 89th chapter of the Qur'an engraved
above the Great Gate of the Taj Mahal.

In the Persian/Urdu script the word for garden is the same as
the word for paradise. It is thought that Shah Jehan is suggesting
that God speaks thus, i.e. '. . . and enter into His paradise.'

These days the approach to the Taj is down a road that ends
in a large car park to which there is no alternative. At the park
one can take an electric mini bus or horse drawn carriage or
rickshaw. The journey is very short and one is deposited outside
the boundary at the ticket booth. Once one has obtained the
ticket then the path takes one forward into the huge enclosed
courtyard area where people have to queue for entrance which is
controlled for security purposes. In the afternoon sunshine this
was no great problem until we saw the size of the queue and
despaired. Anyway we joined it and actually it moved quite
quickly, but I observed others jumping the queue and was highly
indignant. However on my second visit four months later that is
exactly what I was able to do which made me feel guilty, but the

- 87 -

The beautiful red stone Gateway to the Taj Mahal at sunrise.

The Taj Mahal in the afternoon sunlight.

reason is that on the first occasion we had not met up with our guide through a slight misunderstanding. The second time around I went straight to the hotel to meet him and then go to Taj. The security search is a good thing but I doubt they would actually detect anyone seriously determined to damage. As I emerged from the gateway I was nervous that I would feel underwhelmed and disappointed, but it was not so. For all the pictures and all the words the Taj Mahal has its own special serene beauty, and the hot frustration that I had felt at queuing melted away and I just gazed. Of course there were hundreds of people but apart from the odd irritation they did not spoil the experience. In fact we delighted in so many Indians visiting their great national treasure. We remained for as long as possible and I would urge people to make more than one visit. The atmosphere alters with the changing light; see it in sunshine, then at sunset and if possible as we did at sunrise.

Built over 21 years (1632–53) and with twenty thousand crafts-men this ultimate symbol of Moghul extravagance was built as a memorial of love by Emperor Shah Jahan for his wife Mumtaz Mahal who died giving birth to their fourteenth child.

The tomb is within a marble monument standing on a raised platform, topped by a huge central dome and four smaller domes. On the corners of the platform stand four lofty decorative tapered minarets so cleverly constructed as to lean slightly to achieve a perfect perspective. The formal gardens are quartered by water courses in the *charbagh* Muslim design. It is surrounded by a high sandstone wall with three gates. On either side of the central platform are identical red sandstone pavilions; that on the left (west) is a mosque, the one on the right is a copy built for the sake of symmetry. The Urdu architectural name was the word *jawab* meaning echo or reply. The mausoleum is constructed from white marble brought from the area between Jodhpur and Jaipur and the entire building is inlaid with semi precious stones such as carnelian, lapis lazuli, red, yellow and brown jasper, turquoise and jade. The carving is quite superb and so intricate and even the carving in the marble panels is so fine and accurate that all the flowers are recognisable, not just stylised emblems. That first afternoon Graham and I were by ourselves, and though on the Tuesday morning we had an excellent guide with whom we had become friends, on that Sunday afternoon it was just wonderful to take one's shoes off, walk on the surrounding plinth and sit on the parapet and look out on the Jamuna and watch the light change gradually. At the mosque devout Muslims said their prayers when the hour approached, but the rest of us just walked around or sat and lingered and drank it in. Then we retreated to the lawn area from where I judged the best sunset pictures would come and they did. Despite the throng we had a restful memorable experience and left reluctantly.

Now I read that the Taj Mahal is endangered by the 10 million visitors annually and the decades of industrial pollution that have taken their toll. Agra is proud of its efforts to control pollution. To western eyes it would seem 'what control and how much effort?' but much more will have to be done and India should not be too proud to ask advice and seek solutions from others faced with the responsibility of conserving world famous tourist

Carved panels on the Taj Mahal relief carving and Pietra Dura work on dado.

sites. It is infuriating for those of us who care to watch whilst bureaucrats make cosmetic gestures. Now on Fridays Taj is closed, apparently to help limit the numbers and to do any restoration work. Having in the same year spent several days in both Florence and Venice, two magnificent cities under tourist siege, it is quite obvious to us all that authorities will have to have the courage to take measures to preserve these world famous sites for posterity. In the case of the Taj Mahal the Indian Government should spend a sizeable amount on cleaning up Agra and maintaining it as a showcase city with Taj as its jewel. If they are frightened of loss of revenue they are mistaken. Were serious measures implemented to clean and restore the whole city and preserve Taj, Indian tourism would grow, but not in a cheap fashion. Instead the true travellers and lovers of art and history would visit rather than millions of 'cheap seven days away' visitors who have a rather superficial interest.

Apparently 1999 has been designated 'Visit India Year'. I pray that someone with courage and foresight will speak up and demand a millennium pledge to clean restore and maintain all of India's great architectural history. They have the manpower, and the communication system through television to educate, and I have no doubt would also receive sponsorship that acts as advertising. How wonderful if the youth of India could marshal itself with this resolve.

I have however read a suggestion in the British papers that raising the fee for entry to Taj would help. Yes, it is minimal and that would be a good idea if the revenue was purely used on maintenance of the Taj and its environs, but then the fee should be structured to allow Indians to see their national treasure at a realistic figure relevant to their incomes. Those of us who visit India and continually mentally convert into our own respective currencies find it very cheap, but that is not so for the thousands of ordinary folk who come in their family groups to also enjoy their heritage. Therefore all foreign tourists should be required to pay a figure that is double that paid by the country's inhabitants.

We stayed at the Clarks Shiraz in Agra and found it very

satisfactory. On occasions the management could be rather ineffectual but if one firmly remonstrates they act quickly to rectify
the fault. There is a curious habit that one encounters at Indian
hotel check-in desks. People come up and interrupt one's regis-
tration and conversation and the desk clerk seems to think it in
order. On the second occasion when I stayed at the Shiraz I had
yet another experience of this but decided to firmly and forcefully
tell the clerk what I thought of this behaviour and it worked a
treat, and what is more the offending gentleman actually apologised. It could be that Indians because of their heavily populated
country have so little personal space when outside their respective
homes that they do not see this behaviour as offensive. I resolved
that I would not let people invade my personal space whatever
the reason.

The Shiraz has some bedrooms with a beautiful view of Taj
and I was fortunate to have one of these the second time. The
gardens are pleasant and the swimming pool is a welcome relief
in the hot weather as I was to experience in March. There is also
the most charming masseuse in the beauty parlour and she does
wonderful massage with herbal *ayurvedic* oils. The food is good
with a choice of several restaurants and room service. It is quite
interesting to visit a place both as a tourist and then again on
business. I noted the second time that when I had entertained
some people at the poolside and then said goodbye to them and
was wanting to settle the bill the waiter was very surly. I realised
that in fact he was showing his snobbishness and had felt that I
was consorting with people beneath the social order that usually
frequented the hotel. This was unacceptable so I told him in no
uncertain terms never to approach me again without a salver on
which the bill lay instead of just handing it to me, and I told his
manager that I was not impressed with his supervision. If this
sounds over the top it is not. Because of all the hierarchical
intricacies and caste system plus the snob element brought in by
westerners and the relic of the British rule it is vital to treat staff
with courtesy and friendliness, but if they overstep the mark in
any way show firm command of the situation.

Particularly for a woman doing business in India this is essential otherwise respect will evaporate and exploitation take over. In any country in the world people are apt to look for a vulnerable area to exploit, but in India where there is still huge chauvinism and male dominance women should be alert to the necessity of maintaining respect. It is therefore essential that one dresses appropriately – how often did I hear the sneering asides in Hindi from Indian youths when they saw a scantily clad western girl with her bottom hanging out of her brief shorts and her chest visible through a see-through blouse. 'Eve-teasing' is the term used to describe harassment of women and a lot of this has arisen from the multitudes watching western films with all their sexual candour. Our Indian friends think that Bollywood with its gratuitous violence endlessly depicting rape, followed by savage murder and bloodbaths, have led to the huge increase in the crime rate and most especially of rape. Most Indians sadly agree that India is a much more violent place now than thirty years ago.

The following day Anil Sharma our guide took us to the Red Fort. This is well maintained and so impressive. Anil was a

The Red Fort at Agra.

knowledgeable man and with enthusiasm instructed us in its history. The Red Fort at Agra is so much more impressive than that of Delhi, though possibly that is the fault of the British who in revenge for the 1857 uprising decimated it without any thought for history. Indeed when I consider what we as a race did in our arrogance, or tried to do, if you recall that Lord Bentinck planned to dismantle the Taj and auction bits off!

Those of us in the West talk volubly about pollution but we were the original polluters and looters and though we should invite everyone to learn from our mistakes we cannot afford to sit in judgement without at least finding solutions. Indians are very scornful of Americans particularly when the subject of pollution or exploitation rears its head. Americans are very judgemental about India and reduce most comments apparently to 'well, it was nice but so filthy ...'. Just recently the USA has again declined to cut its own pollution levels yet it is one of the world's great offenders. I encountered quite a number of Americans in my Indian travels and they seemed to view everything in a sad superficial light. As a student of history myself I wondered if it is because they are such a young country comparatively and thus have no national folk memory of culture and history upon which to draw and of which to be proud, thus they frantically travel the world to view its antiquities but quite often miss the depth and vision that is a result of antiquity. It is not fair to generalise, I know, but again and again one meets them in both Europe and the East.

In fact Akbar's fort in Agra shares a number of striking features with that built by Shah Jahan in Delhi – it was evidently the model for the latter. Akbar (1556–1605) was the greatest of all the Moghuls. He came to the throne aged thirteen. He conquered massive new territories including much of Rajasthan, he created a proper administrative system, introduced standard weights and measures, tax structures and a sort of police force. Married to at least seven wives; among them was Jodhbai, you may remember, the daughter of the Maharajah of Amber as he then was, Jaipur not having been established as yet. Quite simply the Red Fort at

Agra is worthy of a whole morning in the company of a good guide.

All Moghuls were capable of patricide and even fratricide as we know with Aurangzeb, but standing in the octagonal tower at the window which overlooks the Taj Mahal on the banks of the Jamuna in the distance one cannot help but feel sorry for Shah Jehan, the old man destined to spend his last eight years as a prisoner of his third son Aurangzeb, looking wistfully at his beloved wife's memorial, even deprived of writing paper and books. Auranzeb murdered the rightful heir Prince Dara Shikoh and presented his severed head on a platter to his father. What must his memories have been. In the *Padshanama* – the Chronicle of the Ruler of all the World – which was his title at the zenith of his power there is an exquisite pictorial record of some of his reign. I was glad that earlier in the year I had been able to go to the Queen's Gallery at Buckingham Palace and see that beautifully presented exhibition. The detail of the painting is superb and so interesting because each one depicts an important event in Shah Jehan's life, from his early days as a prince to his accession and the adult lives of his sons. One can fancifully even imagine the resentment in Aurangzeb's face that his wedding celebration is not as magnificent as his brother Prince Dara Shikoh's because he is not the eldest and favourite son. Prince Dara Shikoh's marriage took place quite soon after the tragic death of Mumtaz Mahal who had been apparently instrumental in the planning of it; that too has a poignancy. The Royal Collection is indeed lucky to have one of the very few copies of the *Padshanama* and apparently the only one to be fully illustrated with a portfolio of 44 illustrations. It was given by the Nawab of Oudh via the British Ambassador to King George III and was overlooked when King George IV gave his late father's collection to the British Museum, thus the Windsor Castle collection still retains it and it was made the subject of a beautiful exhibition to commemorate the 50 years of independence of both India and Pakistan.

After a thorough inspection of the Red Fort we had tea and *gulab jamuns* with Anil at the Fort's café. Without him I doubt we would have ventured into the café but Anil is obviously a friend of the owner and ensured we were given the freshest of sweets and we remarked on how delicious they were. A hoopoe meanwhile started pecking at the lawn very close to us and both of us were delighted. You do not see many of them these days but for each of us growing up in India and Africa they were a familiar sight. Agra has so much to see that it is a question of priorities which inevitably are subjective.

By this time it was midday so we set off for Fatehpur Sikri which is 35 kms south-west of Agra on the Jaipur road. This was the culmination of a dream for me as somehow since a teenager I had been entranced with the idea of the Emperor Akbar. At school in England history was taught quite naturally with Britain as the focal point and I realised that Akbar was a contemporary of Queen Elizabeth I; he and his palace city were objects of fascination to me.

Akbar, despite remaining illiterate throughout his life was truly a man before his time. He very quickly realised, despite his extreme youth, having succeeded his father Humayun after the latter's

Fatephur Sikri near Agra.

death as a result of falling down the stairs from his library, that it was a lifetime's folly to try and subjugate the Hindus in 'Hindustan' and he concentrated on winning their loyalty by benevolence and trust. He had a host of Hindu advisors and administrators and he abolished the *jitzya*, a tax on Hindus that the Muslim rulers had introduced. He became deeply interested in other religions and started dialogues between all religions and provided the opportunity for Muslims, Hindus, Jains, Zoroastrians, Jews and Christians to talk about their fundamental beliefs and differences. Orthodox Muslims must have found it very distressing, but this broad religious tolerance was very helpful politically and his marriages to Rajput princesses ensured that the various Rajput princely houses became very loyal and provided him with the bravest of warriors.

Thus within a peaceful empire the arts, literature and music could begin to flourish. He employed scholars and artists and in his newly created library there were texts from Turkey, Sanskrit chronicles and Latin gospels. The arts were now established and so the emperor turned his attention to architecture.

Fatehpur Sikri with the Panch Mahal to the right.

There was however, the story goes, one vital aspect about which Akbar was desperate: he had as yet been unable to produce a surviving heir and he asked a Sufi mystic, Sheik Salim Chishti, for help, and shortly afterwards his son Jehangir was born. In gratitude Akbar built a massive 7.5 sq. km. administrative capital around the Sufi mystic's home between 1570 and 1582. The palace complex was inhabited for about 16 years and then it is thought that Akbar felt threatened in his kingdom and moved to Lahore, the better able to deal with the threat. There is a myth that the city was abandoned because of a shortage of water, but this is unlikely.

The court historian Abul Fazl wrote: 'Inasmuch as his exalted sons had taken their birth in Sikri and God-knowing spirit of Shaikh Salim had taken possession thereof, his holy heart desired to give outward splendour to this spot which possessed spiritual grandeur ... An order was issued that the superintendent of affairs should erect lofty buildings for the special use of the *Shahinshah.*' Here was erected a huge mosque and courtyard and an intricate palace complex and in time the tomb of Sheikh Salim Chishti. Following Akbar's conquest of Gujarat in 1573 he put a prefix to the name of his new city, i.e. 'Fatehpur', or 'City of Victory'. As the nobles and courtiers took his lead and also built houses in the vicinity it rapidly grew into an impressive new centre. Moreover it is recorded that in its heyday the road between Fatehpur Sikri and Agra was flanked by continuous markets. Indeed English travellers of the time remarked on the size and magnificence, but by 1685 Akbar had transferred his capital to Lahore and by the early 17th century the city was crumbling and returning to vegetation and even the principal buildings were falling into decay. Nevertheless Fatehpur Sikri remains today one of the most remarkable architectural conceptions and is still a bit of a Moghul puzzle.

Anyone visiting should not do so without a guide. They are very knowledgeable and can explain the whole sequence of events and tell one so much about the age and architecture. Of course you could just visit with a reputable guide book but the place comes alive with a guide such as Anil or one of his colleagues.

After enjoying the architecture Graham and I walked in the small garden which is well maintained and in seconds the *mali* was by our side. We had an interesting conversation on the various shrubs, one of which was really quite special as the flower turns into a completely different colour and I am ashamed to say I have forgotten the botanical name which tripped off his tongue, and I mean Latin botanical name! *Malis* (gardeners) are not merely men working in a garden, they are for the most part knowledgeable and have pride in their accomplishments. Congratulate the *mali* if appropriate wherever you are and he will be delighted and take you round the garden be it large or small. My childhood hours were often spent in the company of the *mali* and he always took time to explain things. Father had a small *khurpi* (Indian form of hand tool) made for me and I would earnestly try to help. Something must have worked because I won a prize for my larkspur and cornflowers at one flower show, and some snapdragons at another.

The best time to enjoy Indian's horticultural heritage is about February and March, when the winter spectacle of western flowers looks impressive and the indigenous spring flowering trees are coming into bloom. In the monsoon months there is a paucity of blooms, mostly balsams and zinnias, and of course the extreme heat of the hot weather has killed everything else except perhaps some cannas. At Fatehpur Sikri the *mali* asked me to take a photograph of him and promise to send it to him; this I was able to do by handing it over on a second visit to the area.

On our return to Agra we talked about India and her present day politics. In actual fact Anil talked and we listened to a very worthwhile explanation of what was upsetting the average young family man such as himself, and his aspirations and ambitions were really no different to any of us here at that time of life – stability, financial security, good education for his little one and access to healthcare. He was however interested, being a history graduate, in our recent history so I explained what I could of the last fifty years since the Second World War very briefly and how it had impacted on India. He was intrigued, interpretation of history can be fundamentally different we all know, but some of the finer detail was unknown to him and made events more understandable. The Queen's recent visit and the change to a Labour Government were again the major talking point; he could not understand why the Government would be either so arrogant or so naive as to think the Indo-Pakistan conflict could be settled by a few trite words of encouragement and became impassioned and it soon became clear that he was an adherent of the BJP, the Bhratiya Janata Party, which since March 1998 has become the Government of India, though because of all the horse trading a very ineffectual one.

Akbar's mausoleum is at Sikandra and he began building his own tomb in 1602. It is decorated by Muslim, Hindu and Christian symbols, i.e. the round Hindu cupola, the minarets of Islam and the Christian cross; he was obviously determined to have his religious tolerance in life reflected in his death very wisely. The mausoleum is on the Mathura road 15 kms north of Agra.

Mathura is the birthplace of Lord Krishna and therefore immensely important as a centre of pilgrimage; indeed the whole area is littered with small temples that do not have architectural significance but are associated with key events in the god's life.

The tomb of Itimaud-ud-Daulah is superb. Composed of pure white marble inlaid with precious stones and covered with filigree screens it has an air of fragility. It was built between 1622 and 1628 by Nur Jehan (wife of Jehangir, Akbar's longed for son and successor) for her Persian father Mirza Ghias-ud-Din Beg, and it stands in formal *charbagh* gardens. Lastly there are the Ram Bagh gardens laid out by Emperor Babur in 1528. This is the earliest surviving example of a Moghul garden, but is disappointing now and the authorities should recruit some serious *malis* and allocate funds to renovate it back to its former beauty. Indeed were the Uttar Pradesh Government to decide to clean up Agra and impose restrictions on the building proliferation and sympathetically undertake conservation I am confident the area would become a tourists' *Mecca*, and not something that has to be endured to see the Taj Mahal. Situated on the banks of one of India's sacred rivers the Jamuna, with the wealth of Moghul architecture and history it should really be a huge World Heritage Site and in the winter months could become a destination of delight, whereas at the moment the normal reaction is one of awe at Taj, currently itself a World Heritage Site, but shock and disgust at Agra.

We visited the Taj Mahal again at sunrise and were so grateful for that opportunity. Naturally the crowds are quite minimal if one is early enough and one's patience is rewarded by the sunrise and the possibilities for photography. There are some tiresome people who talk volubly about 'a Diana pose' but it is easy to ignore them and hopefully all that in time will fade away to a sad memory. It is however worthwhile having one of the local photographers take a picture of one as an individual or couple because he will bring the results to the hotel a couple of hours later and they are good and inexpensive. It captures the mood for you at the time when it is still foremost in the mind.

On the way back to our hotel we watched in amusement all the cycle rickshaws weighed down with small children going to school. Yet again they were beautifully dressed and neat and

Aline Dobbie sitting in front of the Taj Mahal during sunrise.

attractive; what alarmed us was the fact that each rickshaw was overcrowded and we worried about possible accidents. That evening to our horror on the national news was the account of a most horrible school bus accident in Delhi in which countless children had died and been injured. The scale of the tragedy was immense, and all due to an aggressive driver at the controls of an overloaded bus – we grieved along with the rest of the country, who were also very angry. It spoilt the end of what had been a superbly interesting day.

If leaving Agra to return to Delhi I would suggest using the Shatabdhi Express which leaves at 8.00 p.m. arriving in Delhi at about 10.30 p.m. It is inexpensive by western standards and efficient; under no circumstances consider returning by car. In my case on both occasions the driver returned to Delhi on his own in the early morning to avoid the danger of night travel. We however on the first occasion were travelling south-east and so that afternoon we flew from Agra to Khajuraho in Madhya Pradesh. The security at Agra airport was intense, and further reinforced by the arrival of the American Secretary of State. In fact the Taj was closed that afternoon for her privileged viewing which must have been hard on the countless tourists who would not have known about that trip in their planning.

CHAPTER ELEVEN

Khajuraho and Madhya Pradesh

The trip to Khajuraho is short and pleasant and it is a superb destination. A small, neat, comparatively clean place with many excellent hotels and just the two sets of temple complexes to visit. Madhya Pradesh is the heartland of India, and literally translated means 'Middle Land'. It is India's largest state and covers approximately 450,000 sq. kms. The next largest state is Rajasthan and that is about 100,000 sq. kms smaller!

Geographically Madhya Pradesh is very diverse. The northern part of the state with Gwalior as its largest city lies in the Indo-Gangetic plain whereas the rest is upland plateau and hills interspersed with deep valleys. Some of the finest of India's forests are in this state with deciduous hardwoods such as teak, sal, Indian ebony and rosewood. Bamboo is prolific and the fruit and flowering trees are wonderful. Rudyard Kipling's famous *Jungle Book* was sited in the Mahadeo Hills of the Satpura Range and here you will find tiger, panther, Indian bison and the whole spectrum of herbivores.

Ashoka, the great Buddhist emperor, had Malwa, the old name for Madhya Pradesh, as the centre of his Mauryan Empire and the most important relics of his reign are at Sanchi where there is a Buddhist centre. This is a small place but well worth a visit for its charm and obvious antiquity but to get there you would need to travel from Bhopal; for us on the recent trip it was not possible and we had to content ourselves with Khajuraho which is easily reached by plane. However on a future occasion we shall add Orchha, Gwalior, Mandu and Pachmarhi to our itinerary. There are also several wildlife reserves here which from recent accounts are worth visiting but travel in the interior of Mahhya Pradesh is not as easy as on the popular tourist trails and the traveller would have to contend with long car and train journeys and be both patient and tolerant and not too demanding about accommodation standards.

Khajuraho has a population of under 10,000, at least that is what my research has discovered, so in Indian terms it is a minute place and comparable to Peebles, our local market town here in the beautiful Borders region of Scotland. Its size makes it a most delightful place to rest and recharge the batteries. The temples are fascinating and well maintained in attractive garden areas and moving around is so easy with so little traffic. I imagine given more time cycling would have been attractive. We stayed at the Jass Oberoi which was both elegant and comfortable with very nice staff. The grounds are beautifully maintained with a delightful pool and sitting area and one can see why Khajuraho has become a honeymoon venue for young couples or a weekend destination since the other hotels are equally well appointed. Because Khajuraho is difficult to get to other than by plane the airline seats are reserved well in advance and sadly there is not yet sufficient competition in India's internal airlines to challenge the somewhat mixed reputation and monopoly of Indian Airlines.

Khajuraho was once a great Chandela capital this was a dynasty that lasted for five centuries before falling to the Moghul onslaught. The temples almost all date from a burst of creativity that started in AD 950 and lasted one hundred years. The puzzle is why? Khajuraho as we have seen is difficult to get to so was presumably even more difficult a thousand years ago and though charming does not appear to have any special quality as a venue for massive temple construction. Moreover in the hot weather it is extremely hot and dry and dusty. For us seeing it all on a pleasant couple of days in the cool of November almost gives a false impression,

Khajuraho Temples.

but one with which we were very content. Possibly because of its remoteness the Muslims did nothing to destroy what in the early days of Muslim invasion was regarded as 'idolatrous' and for that we must be grateful.

With a good guide you will see the carvings as a celebration of all aspects of life, not simply erotica. In fact it is believed to have been the depiction of *Tantric* life in which sexual activity can be used to eliminate the evils of the world and achieve final deliverance. The quest for *nirvana Rhoa* which is physical enjoyment is rated as highly as yoga which is spiritual exercise. Our guide was a very serious young man and he had found that the way to have a discourse on these matters in the presence of women was to talk whilst looking at the carvings and then looking down, i.e. not catching my eye. Since there are some very saucy depictions it seemed a satisfactory way to conduct matters! Had Graham and I been alone I am sure we would have had a good giggle. However

Amazing carvings on Khajuraho Temples.

Khajuraho Temple carvings in exquisite detail.

the guide was almost apoplectic when he overheard what another guide was putting forth; I don't know what so enraged him but he had a quiet tirade on the dangers of exploitative guides who told innocent westerners a lot of nonsense.

The temples comprise the Western, the Eastern and the Southern groups and they are easy to walk around and contemplate and photograph. I was not so much interested in the erotic positions of humans as the delicacy of the carving of some of the female attire and little details of the maidenly conceit, plus the roguish look in the eyes of some of the animals like the elephants and camels.

We were scheduled to fly onto Varanasi but had we had the time I should have liked to visit the Kanha National Park about 32 kms away and the Ajaigarh and Kalinjar fort which are about 80 kms from Khajuraho. The former was a Chandela building but the latter Kalinjar is much much older, built during the Gupta period and technically inside Uttar Pradesh.

Just as we had settled down beside the pool to have a rest and some lunch fate took a hand and we saw the little man who was the local representative of our travel agent approaching. He announced that there was an airport controllers' strike and thus our flight was very delayed and rather uncertain. We were dismayed. If we did not return to Delhi by the morning our continuing schedule would be affected and there was something important that we needed to accomplish in Delhi. We asked Badli Alu to do his utmost to make sure we were on the next aircraft when it arrived. In the meantime I began to notice that the hotel lobby was filling up with impatient looking Americans. It occurred to us that if all the people who were now milling around in our hotel wanted to embark on the same aircraft, plus similar numbers in the other hotels, life would become rather stressed and hectic, and someone would have to lose out! I determined it would not be us so went and asked for a telephone. Naturally several other people had the same idea and very soon the telephone lines to Delhi were jammed. In the meantime I heard the local agent who was senior to Badli in managerial rank having a telephone conversation I asked him to please ensure we were able to leave. His attitude was unattractive, but as I was speaking in English he had no knowledge of my Hindi and so when he started a conversation and told the person at the airline end of the telephone that he would fob some of us off I simply 'phoned the Delhi head office and explained very angrily what I had heard. This can happen in India, and even the people you least expect to let you down or deceive you will do so. They are inclined to tell you what you want to hear, regardless of the consequences and that you will in turn discover their deception. I made it clear that any nonsense would have serious repercussions with the managing director. If it sounds like one person jumping up and down having a tantrum, it is, but without the jumping up and down!

It all became quite funny as time wore on because we could all hear the little aircraft arrive and then take off – apparently the same one which had flown from Delhi to Agra, then Khajuraho and on to Varanasi then back to Khajuraho then back to Agra, return to Khajuraho and once more to Varansi and so forth! By the late evening the Jass Oberoi very kindly laid on a buffet supper and young Badli Alu who was by this time worn out came back to assure us we were on the next flight but having to go to Varanasi and then to Delhi.

Badli looked exhausted and when we asked when if at all he had eaten he said at about 5.00 a.m. prior to going to work. He lived some way away and his young wife was at her parents' house with their firstborn (which is the customary way for young first time mothers in India). I said he must have something to eat and he was very embarrassed. Again it was the case of the lower class, with insufficient status to even think of eating in the Jass. 'Enough,' I said, 'you will be our guest and everything else can wait,' and I ordered him a bar meal of his rather shy choice with tea and cool drinks for us. The barman looked down his nose and made very little effort to progress the order so I went to the bar and said in Hindi that this was my order for my guest and he better believe it! The meal arrived and the young man wolfed it down despite his shyness. He was so humble and so eager to please and he did his utmost to ensure everything else went smoothly. However, Graham and decided that as we were independent travellers despite Badli's assurances we would go to the little airport in good time, not totally trusting the airline clerks who with an innocent stare may well have switched the names around were we to turn up at the appointed time. Our hunch paid off, and we also positioned ourselves near the door of the transit lounge. True to form, the clerks had given up on the problem and issued everyone with a boarding pass, but there were no allocated seats. I have never seen so many middle aged American, German, Japanese tourists swarm to the narrow door and all try to get out at the same time. Graham and I had worked it out and were a little ahead of the game. Thankfully we sat ourselves in the first pair of seats near the rear door.

When that aircraft revved its engines and started its take-off truly I prayed to my own God, Lord Ganesha in the Hindu deity and the Sufi Saint of Fatehpur Sikri. It somehow felt as if the little machine was totally exhausted and not wanting to leave the ground – oh, I know this was fanciful but it really felt like that sitting in the extreme rear of the aircraft! The flight to Varansi was uneventful and after refuelling we were thankfully on our way having flown about 1000 kms out of our way. We arrived at Delhi's internal airport at midnight totally exhausted but thankful, and were met by Ajay and Balvinder Singh. We were taken to the United Services complex where they operate a sort of hotel rather like a military mess. There are no frills but it is clean and the staff are pleasant and the whole complex is very interesting, as we discovered once we had had a good night's sleep.

CHAPTER TWELVE

Delhi in Diverse Detail

W̲ithin the last twelve months I had been able to spend nearly
three weeks in Delhi but fortunately spread out through
three of the seasons beginning with our November visit, followed
on in March and culminating in May. Winter in which we first
arrived is the most pleasant season in Delhi, sunny and cool, but
the minimum temperature drops sharply in late December and
January and every time there is a heavy snowfall in the mountains
icy winds blow down from the north. In March there is a brief
change of season between winter and the hot weather. Spring lasts
only a few weeks in February and March but it is attractive because
it is the season of new leaf – many of Delhi's indigenous forest
trees are covered in vivid green and this is followed by the vibrant
colour of the ornamental flowering trees. The Hindu festivals of
Basant Panchami and *Holi* celebrate this season, known in Hindi
as *Basant*.

In the Indian tradition there are six seasons – *Grishma, Varsha,
Sharad, Hemant, Sheet* and *Basant*. They correspond approximately
to Summer, Rains, Post rains, Early winter, Winter and Spring.
The most famous literary work on the theme of seasons is the
Ritusamhara, literally the gathering of seasons written in the 5th
century by the Sanskrit poet Kalidasa. The credit for planting
indigenous forest species in Delhi is shared between Lutyens, the
architect of New Delhi and William Robertson Mustoe, who came

Lutyen's New Delhi.

to India in 1919 from London's Kew Gardens. Indeed just this summer the Royal Botanical Gardens of Edinburgh held an exhibition of exquisite paintings of Indian trees in bloom with meticulous line drawings showing the early discoveries by the various plantsmen who went to India and began the great plant collections for the various botanical gardens and private estates. The Calcutta Botanical Gardens which in their time were superb were featured as were the Agri-Horticultural Gardens of Calcutta where so much early work was trailed.

It was a pleasure to see again the gulmohur flower in shades of fire red and orange, the bauhinia in delicate mauve, the laburnum festooned with racemes of gold, the jacaranda which becomes a delicate filigree of mauve and blue, the champak or temple tree which has exquisitely textured and scented flowers and interspersed with all these the ancient pipals, the most common of the ficus (fig) species, and the neem. Neem provides dense shade and its medicinal and germicidal properties have been known for centuries but have recently come to the attention of the West. In places like Bareilly we were able to briefly walk in orchards of mangoes and guavas, though it was not the season for fruit, and there too were the *lagerstroemia* or Pride of India with blooms in shades of deep pink or mauve, and closer to winter the rusty shieldbearer or *peltophorum roxburghi* stands out with its copper-red oblong seed pods and sprays of yellow touched with rust flowers.

In the third week of February it is customary for the Moghul Garden at Rashtrapati Bhawan, the Residence of the Indian President (previously the viceroy's palace) to be opened to the public for about two weeks and this is beautiful, but the inevitable security checks have to be endured.

The building of New Delhi created a garden city but wisely did not tamper with the old parks and thus it is possible to see some of the old garden remains from centuries before. Now however, fifty years on from independence, Delhi's population has grown hugely and it is now a megalopolis. I have heard the figure 30 million used in conjunction with Delhi and its various satellite towns like Gurgaon, Noida, Ghaziabad, Shadara, Faridabad and Rohini. This has put a severe strain on civic amenities and the environment and the power utilities.

I had been told that when Indira Gandhi was in power she had decreed that Delhi was never to be without power and water. It is the capital of India, and of that the country should be justifiably proud and therefore even if it meant taking from the other interstate electricity grids the capital was never to be deprived of power. Sadly because of that arrangement not enough has been done to provide Delhi with sufficient electricity and water when the hot season arrives and this year there were large demonstrations with hundreds if not thousands of Delhi residents showing their frustration and displeasure.

It is so foolish to just keep trying to 'make do'. India has huge talent in scientific and engineering skills. If a courageous government would just commission new environmentally friendly forms of power stations and provision for water very probably the rest of the world would help them financially, provided that whoever was appointed in charge of such huge building projects had sufficient integrity and complete authority to oversee it without corruption. Indians become very defensive about their massive environmental problems, but they need not be. It seems to me that all of us in the West are only too aware of the logistical problems they face, but it requires honesty and with honesty and integrity they will clothe themselves in dignity, which is quite naturally important to the nation as a whole. When I left India thirty five years ago there were about 500 million people; now it is one billion. To see beautiful Delhi under such strain is heart-breaking and there are no easy solutions, but face-saving cosmetic legislation provides no lasting solution.

We were fortunate enough to stay at the India International Centre in both March and May as temporary members. It was visualised as an international centre for exchange of ideas among scholars. The architect was J. A. Stein and he built a typical 1960s building but it captured the soft quality of light through the use of traditional *jaalis* (screens). There is a library, an auditorium, conference rooms, restaurants and a beautiful garden.

J. A. Stein was also responsible for the Ford Foundation building in 1968, the Memorial Plaza, the Lodi Greenhouse, UNICEF Headquarters, the World Wide Fund for Nature – India, and the India Habitat Centre as recently as 1994.

The great advantage of staying in such a charming club-like institution is that one is able to see Indians at work and leisure. If you are in the very sophisticated five-star hotels, beautiful as they, are the predominant hotel guests are foreigners. In the International Centre it is quite the reverse and very nice too. There is now a recent annexe which is equally well thought out with its own restaurants and theatres. The food in the various dining rooms and lounges is good and inexpensive and it makes it much easier to entertain for business and pleasure. In May we had a lovely suite with its own balcony, sitting room, bedroom area and bathroom overlooking the Lodi Garden.

The garden was laid out around the beautiful tombs of the Lodi and Sayyid sultans who ruled north India in the 15th and 16th centuries. There used to be a village where the garden now exists but it was relocated in 1936 when the garden was then called Lady

India International Centre – New Delhi.

Willingdon Park. It was renamed Lodi Garden in 1947 and was re-landscaped by J. A. Stein and Garrett Eckbo in 1968. Depending on the season the garden is very pleasant. In January and February and perhaps March the flower beds are full of English country garden flowers but by May the heat is intense and only the flowering trees and shrubs give colour. It is a favourite garden for Delhi picnickers, mothers with babes in prams and the jogging fraternity. Early in the morning before the heat takes over we would observe the earnest Delhi joggers or walkers of all ages. We decided to join them but at a very leisurely walk. The scene was attractive and interesting – the young perhaps using the opportunity for flirtation, the military types walking in stern fashion, whole families out to take the air, humble youths playing simple cricket – all this going on daily around the tomb of Mohammed Shah who died in 1444, or the Bara Gumbad and Masjid erected in 1494 and the Sheesh Gumbad which is decorated with tiles in two shades of blue giving it a glazed appearance. That same blue pottery is still made in Delhi by one family nowadays, Hazarilal

Lodi Tombs in Lodi Gardens in cultural New Delhi.

– we have a most beautiful lamp in the classic shape and a vase and plate to match. Those items are only 40 years old, bought by my parents, but it is amazing to think that they are being manufactured in the same way as those tiles of centuries ago. A special mix of powdered quartz is used to make the stoneware base which is then glazed blue, with ingredients which were used for the pre-Moghul and Moghul domes. The tomb of Sikander Lodi 1517 resembles Mohammed Shah's tomb but there are no *chattris* along the dome. Each morning when I walked out of the International Centre's gates into the Lodi Garden there was an extraordinary feeling that here I was in modern New Delhi built by the last great imperial invaders but if I looked through the early sun's rays I would catch a glimpse of folk who had lived and worked in the intervening centuries since the tombs had been built five hundred years ago.

There is so much to see in Delhi that it would take a stay of several weeks to do it justice. Critics of Delhi dismiss it and say that it should be just a jumping off place, but that is usually extreme youth in its arrogance and ignorance talking.

Indraprastha in 1400 BC was the ancient Delhi on the banks of the Jamuna, the legendary Pandavas of the Mahabharata are said to have ruled from here in the eastern part of the city. The last Hindu kingdom in north India was ruled from an area in South Delhi. Delhi remained a capital city almost throughout the period between 1190 and 1526, of a state whose boundaries kept shifting and which include Afghanistan and the Deccan. The Mamluks were succeeded by Khaljis, Tughlaqs, Sayyids and Lodis.

Not only was Delhi the site of royal power but after the fall of Baghdad in 1358 when the Caliphate shifted to Cairo, it became the capital of Islam in India. Along with Ajmer in Rajasthan it was a major centre for Sufism – a popular form of Islam which came close to Hindu mysticism.

Delhi's architecture and opulence was famous and breathtaking in the medieval world and it became a magnet for all – merchant adventurers, devout pilgrims – and marauders like Timur. In 1398 Timur and his armies ransacked Delhi – in similar fashion to the actions of the Crusaders in Constantinople in 1204.

Vasco de Gama, the ultimate merchant adventurer, was to land on India's shores at Calicut and the Portugese proceeded to behave in a barbaric fashion in the name of Christendom; that was exactly five hundred years ago. Thirty years later Babur of Samarkand, descendant of Timur and Genghis Khan, challenged Ibrahim Lodi and was successful. Babur's diary is a most valuable document because he details his opinions of the newly conquered land and writes with complete candour and in some detail. His description of the elephant which hitherto he had not encountered is enchanting, as are his details on the fauna and flora of 'Hindustan'. The Moghuls as we have seen were an immensely successful dynasty, but by the 18th century the empire began to crumble following the death of Bahadur Shah in 1712.

The Maratha Empire followed stretching to the north and east from the deccan, but by 1750 they too had been defeated by Afghan invaders. by the end of the century the Rajputs turned to Britain to help rid themselves of the Marathas, and thus British Rule came into existence. The Regulating Act turned the East

India Company into a British administrative agency and Warren Hastings was appointed the first Governor-General of British India. By 1815–18 the Marathas had finally been vanquished and almost the entire subcontinent was now under the direct rule of the British. In 1857–58 the Indian Mutiny, or as I prefer to call it, First Indian Revolt took place, sparked off by a false rumour that bullets were greased with cow and pig fat thus offending both Hindu and Muslim soldiers. The Rajputs allied themselves to the British and after intense fighting, with severe atrocities committed by both sides the British finally won.

In the mid-19th-century imperial arrogance and ignorance were equal partners and though lessons were said to have been learnt, Indians were to continue to feel the yolk of the overlord. In 1877 Queen Victoria was proclaimed Empress of India and from that moment India was governed by a viceroy and an Indian Council. In 1885 The Indian National congress held its first meeting and the seeds of the movement to free India from British imperial rule were sewn.

The British had changed the capital from Delhi to Calcutta but

Raj Ghat Ghandiji's Memorial.

in 1911 the decision to return to Delhi and construct a whole new imperial capital was taken and Sir Edwin Lutyens was commissioned to design and build the capital fit for an Empire. This was in line with the building that had taken place in South Africa and other Dominions.

Fifty years after independence Delhi is a teeming city state, fully mindful of the seven cities that have gone before but full of their legacy and now interacting with the whole world. Countries vie with each other to gain a market share for their respective manufacturers, others send their skilled engineers to persuade the government that they too should be allowed a manufacturing base within the subcontinent; world renowned designers fly to India to find inspiration for their next season's collections, and professional bodies invariably find Delhi an exotic venue in which to hold world conferences, be they on human medicine, veterinary medicine or other world encompassing topics.

Waking up one morning in March feeling incredibly weary from an overnight journey I heard the muezzin's call from the great Jama Masjid (Friday Mosque). For one night I was staying at the Park Hotel and therefore within range of the sound. It reinvigorated me and as I looked out of the window I saw the wheeling flocks of pigeons swoop and fly in circles with the sound of the muezzin floating like a benediction across this great teeming place. It filled me with hope for Delhi and for India – some things never change, God willing, and that continuity will always bring strength to a vital people who will find a way to go forward building on the centuries of heritage.

As I have already said there is so much to see but the way to do it is to pace oneself and if time permits arrange for a guide and hire a car with driver which works out cheaper and a great deal more convenient than endlessly hailing a taxi. Moreover, should a shopping excursion present itself then the shopping can be safely stowed in the car until the frenzy has passed! Frankly you could shop until you drop, but seriously there are so many wonderful things to buy – Kashmiri carpets, fabrics from all over the subcontinent, jewellery, brass and silverware, leather goods, *objets d'art* across the spectrum from simple village to gallery sophistication, artwork, books, furniture that can be shipped overseas and clothes. Nowadays an immense proportion of the world's clothes for both genders are manufactured in India and sold under well known brand names in western countries, and probably the east as well. On our journey to Bareilly we met two young men who were quality controllers for leather and brassware travelling to Moradabad, the large city one stop before Bareilly. It seems that Uttar Pradesh has become the manufacturing base for all the wrought iron work that is currently so fashionable along with the metal/aluminium look in the West, and Saharanpur further north in the same state is a centre for furniture made out of *sheesham* wood. As a child in the 1950s I had lived in Saharanpur so the idea that exporting to the West has brought prosperity to the local artisans is a happy thought.

Eating out in Delhi is also an adventure and visits to the various five star hotel restaurants can be very enjoyable. We particularly enjoyed the Bukhara and the Dum Phukt in the Maurya Sheraton – the food was outstanding in attractive surroundings. Way over in South Delhi there is the Village Bistro which is a huge complex of eight restaurants including Continental, South Indian, North Indian, Chinese and kebab and *tandoori* specialities. Lunchtime is very well catered for by the Imperial which is so central and has the added advantage of Thomas Cook to hand; besides, what could be nicer than sitting out on the hotel's terrace overlooking the green lawns on a winter's afternoon. Inside there is an Indian buffet and much entertainment to be had just ear bending to the various tables around one where so often parliamentarians are thrashing out some political strategy. In November we were fascinated by the horse trading going on at the table next to us and as the Government was in danger of falling it was doubly intriguing. An election was called very soon after that occasion. At the Santushti shopping complex originally started by military officers' wives there is the Basil and Thyme bistro. This is a very popular lunchtime venue where the young and fashion conscious like to be seen.

The shopping complex itself is at the sophisticated end of the spectrum and interesting in a beautiful garden setting.

Best of all however is the warm hospitality extended by Indians, old friends or new acquaintances. Anybody can travel the world and view each new place from the poolside or shopping mall of a glamorous hotel, but to begin to understand a country it requires visiting in the homes of the locals. I have happy memories of several such visits across the social spectrum.

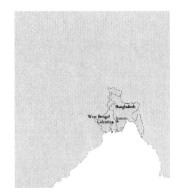

CHAPTER THIRTEEN

Calcutta and Memory Lane

Graham and I flew on to Calcutta, arriving at night, but on my second trip I arrived in the early morning sunshine and was able to see this vast city sprawling beneath me. Much has changed, and only some of it is an improvement. There are new road systems which curiously serve to condense the distances, or is it that my teenage memories have distorted the reality? – a bit of both I suspect. We were on both occasions guests of dear friends Monu and Champak Basu and I had last entered their house in March 1963. It was as elegant as ever but they had made some minor changes upon which I commented. Champak seemed amazed that I should recall it so clearly. They had visited us in Edinburgh in 1996 and been special guests at my mother's 85th birthday, but it was lovely to catch up with them in their own surroundings and I looked forward to meeting Srila again and seeing their little granddaughters for the first time. Like all close families the grandchildren play an important part in their lives and the family circle brings that special relaxation. The youngest granddaughter was to celebrate her fifth birthday on our last full day and preparations were busy and fraught. The little one was to be dressed in a new dress especially ordered by her *Nani* and to prevent her elder sister feeling left out *Nani* was hurriedly making a matching skirt – this suddenly became a last minute problem because a chubby seven year old does not have a defined waist line, but frantic improvisations were a success. Early in the morning we sat and drank tea on the first floor terrace surrounded by exotic blooms with the calls of the various hawkers floating up to us and Calcutta's snarling traffic already making its presence felt. In the east the early morning is a special time and a quiet cup of tea and glance at the *Statesman* – Calcutta's national newspaper – was a pleasant way to relax and chat.

Calcutta was a British creation. The exhibition at the Victoria Memorial takes one through from its creation to the present day. Job Charnock stepped ashore from his ship in 1690 having sailed down the river from Hoogly which was the little port and factory site for the East India Trading Company. He chose the area between three villages, Kalikata, Govindapur and Sutanuti, as the new site for the enlarged factory for the company, and thus was Calcutta born. It therefore has none of Delhi's antiquity and heritage, and though it went on to become the capital of India, second city of the Empire and a world centre it went into decline after World War II. Today it strikes one as a city in decay and sadly so many of the fine buildings of a century ago are being allowed to crumble and add to the air of decrepitude.

With Partition at Independence Calcutta had to withstand the onslaught of hundreds of thousands of refugees from what was East Pakistan and then again as a result of the Indo-Pakistan conflict of 1971 and the creation of Bangla Desh when it broke away from Pakistan. It was already suffering from a population explosion but this was to deal it a body blow and put the city's utilities under severe strain. However, it appears that some of these problems have been overcome and in many ways Calcutta enjoys a stability that places like Delhi do not. Nor should one endlessly harp on about its disadvantages because Calcutta, though a city of over 12 million people, has a warmth and friendliness about it that is recognised throughout the subcontinent.

Kipling rather sneeringly wrote:

From the midday halt of Charnock ... More's the pity grew a city,
as fungus spreads chaotic, from its bed so it spread, Chance directed,

chance erected laid and built on the silt. Palace, pyre, hovel, poverty and pride Side by side ...

(Rudyard Kipling, *A Tale of Two Cities*)

There is now a metro and a second Howrah Bridge to compliment the original built in 1941 by the British. Some said that the Victoria Memorial was built to rival the Taj Mahal; well, it does not in any way do that, yet it stands imposing and serene with its reflections mirrored in the surrounding ornamental pools on a sunny day. I had never entered it before and found the present exhibition well presented. It was encouraging to see so many local visitors and in fact we were the only Europeans present and thus

The Memorial to Queen Victoria in Calcutta, West Bengal.

asked to pose with numerous groups and families for photographs. This building had also held a fascination for me but when I was a child it had nothing of worth inside to encourage a visit, I was told. Indeed, Mother recalls vividly how it had to be camouflaged during the war to prevent Japanese bomber pilots using it as a marker in their raids over the Kidderpore docks a few miles away. I had heard that serious renovations of the various oil paintings in the interior are being undertaken and this will enhance a fine building. Indians are mature and now with a half century past since independence see the relics of British imperialism in their perspective. I truly hope so and I do hope they will conserve the other buildings around BBD Bagh.

For me Calcutta is a place of family history. My paternal grandparents were married in the Roman Catholic chapel of Fort William, which today is still a military establishment though I believe the chapel is now a library; my maternal grandparents were married in the Scots Kirk of St Andrew in Dalhousie Square. Grandfather Ord had been an elder and was the treasurer to the kirk session. My own parents were also married in St Andrew's, three days prior to Father going off to war in the Malayan campaign. My own confirmation took place in the Cathedral of St Paul's by the Metropolitan Bishop of India, Burma and Ceylon in April 1961. This building was consecrated in 1847 and is in a gothic style painted a pale shade of grey. The steeple fell during an earthquake in 1897 and there was further damage in the 1934 quake and it had to be rebuilt. St Paul's is still very much in use but sadly St Andrew's is only opened about twice a year for services. My mother sometimes indulges nostalgia by visiting the Kirk of St Andrew and St George in Edinburgh's George Street as this was the model for that church so far away which is its exact replica with curved interior and elegant simplicity. Were she to go back to Calcutta there would be too many ghosts. My maternal grandparents are buried in the now famous Park Street cemeteries as are other relatives, but that was a pilgrimage from which I refrained. The sepia photographs of them in my family album are altogether happier reminders.

As a girl I would ride my pony, Miss Muffet, on the Maidan (great stretch of green) and then canter or gallop round the Race Course. Very often the Commissioner for Calcutta Police, Mr P K Sen, would kindly ask me to accompany him. In my mind's eye I see a small pigtailed girl astride a bay mare, keeping up gamely with a large man confidently riding a huge magnificent black horse called Fujiyama. Because of his status those around would wish and show deference but 'PK' would chat to me and encourage me to ride without a saddle to enhance my horsemanship. After these early morning rides PK would presumably go off to his office and I would go home to bathe and change and go to school. Sometimes if it was a holiday my mother would suggest we go to Fleury's for breakfast and this was a huge treat. Fleury's still exists but I think in a different form. In the '50s and '60s it was the place to go for coffee or tea and cakes and pastries and savouries. Moreover the Swiss manager with his charming jovial manner would be only too pleased to make special birthday cakes and tiny marzipan figures with which to grace a birthday table. Calcutta in those days could produce the most memorable *Sachertorte* or other delectable patis-serie and the detail of the icing and marzipan work could rival anything in Vienna or Geneva! Very often dinner party hostesses did not even try to concoct sumptuous desserts, they just went in advance to Fleury's and could be confident of a showstopper!

Club life is very lively in Calcutta and it was a pleasure to once again sample the freshness of Tollygunge. How many times have I swum in that old fashioned pool and then sunned myself on the racecourse outside? In those days Tollygunge had its own small racecourse and it was possible to have tea on the lawn, play golf and watch horse-racing all at the same time, Oh! and have a game of tennis as well if the opportunity arose. Sometimes it seems that was the end of an era, but like all of life it has simply evolved and now the well-to-do Indians are all, I am glad to say, doing similar things. Calcutta needs these distractions as it is a cultural city but with little opportunity for rural leisure. The city and country clubs give an opportunity for relaxation and socialising. Golf is now a major status sport.

In other aspects of life there is also continuity. The little Basu granddaughters attend school at La Martinière, a private establishment, and that is where my mother started her school life before going back to Britain in the 1920s. Before I left India for boarding school in Winchester I attended Miss Scrimshaw's in Alipore and then Miss Martin George in Camac Street. Indeed I recall vividly writing my 11+ exam for entry to Saint Swithun's in the classroom of the nursery folk. Miss Martin George was quite a martinet and very annoyed with me subsequently. The English paper asked the pupil to describe the room in which he or she was seated for the examination. I did just that, but with a child's no nonsense eye described it without frills. Miss Martin George had through middle age lost the ability to see the room with its peeling wall pictures and shabby schoolroom furniture; she presumably still saw it in its pristine colours of yesteryear! Now in Camac Street there is another school, I believe run by the Charity Future Hope. In this school no-one is privileged or returning home at the end of the school day to parental mansions of affluence. The pupils are gathered from the street children of Calcutta and it is the brainchild of Tim and Erica Grandage. Through education to be able to change the aspirations of some of these children who have been hardened by the harshness and deprivation of their lives is a wonderful opportunity and one I would dearly love to help. The Grandages have registered their charity in Britain and operate from a London address in W11.

Calcutta does not require intense sight-seeing though for the energetic there is plenty to choose from, but for me it was a journey of nostalgia and such happy memories. Yes, it is a shabby, decrepit overpopulated city but there are still some rare instances of great beauty and special experiences.

We required to buy a birthday present and where else to go than the New Market, formerly the Sir Stewart Hogg Market. This is a huge sprawling conglomeration of shops under cover. Part of it was burnt down in 1985 but happily it was rebuilt. In childhood a visit to the New Market was always an exciting way to spend a couple of hours. Now seen through the eyes of a well travelled mature adult it still has charm, but one would need to be very selective. However, everything you could possibly ever want is on sale in different shops which are laid out rather like a European indoor market in France or Italy. As you leave the car a porter or (coolie) approaches – I signalled my acceptance of him and said that we needed a toy shop. The man strode ahead and I followed with Graham bringing up the rear. Unknown to me he was thinking, 'Fancy Aline remembering the way after all this time ...' I had not of course but was confident of our leader! At the toy shop we inspected everything with the help of two assistants and finally decided on a globe. Having made the purchase I put it into the coolie's basket and Graham queried it and said he would carry the item and tried courteously to dispense with the man. I explained that that was not how things are done and to trust me. After toys we wanted the florist's; I would try to find the flower shop where my mother used to shop and have them make a bouquet of flowers for Champak. We were led to the arcade of flowers and duly ordered the bouquet, comprising gladi-oli in subtle shades. Gladioli are very popular in Indian flower markets all over the country but I would not allow any old mixture of colours. This required time and care. The three of us stood waiting and watching the preparation.

I was beginning to wilt from the heat and humidity and the coolie and I had a conversation which ranged round my childhood, parents and now my own children. I said that they were now grown men in their twenties and that I missed them. Then transpired a superb monologue – it would be generous to describe it as a dialogue. The old coolie said of course that was the way of life, children are precious but they grow up and become men but in your heart they are always your babies. So much I under-stood but my rusty inadequate vocabulary was letting me down. I found all that he said so moving and translated for Graham who agreed vigorously with gestures and several 'Hahs'. He talked about Calcutta and his life and then when we left for the car he naturally followed with our purchases. He bade me look for him again when I come and that he would see me. We parted with that spontaneous affection that can just happen in India and I gave him what I hoped was a generous tip – it apparently was. All around the poor were begging – young girls, old women, mothers with babes in arms – we tried to give something but truly one needs a bottomless purse and that we do not have. We returned to the Basu home contented with our outing but troubled by all we saw around us. However, some superb home cooking and pleasant relaxed conversation after a much needed shower was very enjoyable.

Calcutta still has Armenian and Chinese communities tucked away in little corners of the city centre. Somehow they cling to their ancestral identities and cultures. The Armenians were a large community in my youth and several well to do children were in prep school with me. A huge proportion of the Armenians seem to work as railway drivers and management, and craftsmen. The Chinese continue as they have always done but I think their standing was affected by the Indo-Chinese war of November 1962 which I clearly recall. Certainly the Chinese hairdresser that we all went to in the early 1960s very near to the New Market was discovered to be a listening post for the Chinese Government and the owner and some of her girls were arrested. Since I was only sixteen at the time I was duly very impressed with the idea that my hair had been dressed by a spy! Images of black and white movies with Trevor Howard admonishing one that 'careless talk cost lives' came to mind.

In March there was a curious feeling I experienced that I was part onlooker and part player in an Indian game. I was in Calcutta on business and required some legal advice. Having been driven to the building near the High Court I had to make my way through the throng on the pavement and find the right office on the fifth floor. It was astonishing. The sheer magnitude of the crowd, the endless hawking, talking, bargaining going on all around me. The lift was under pressure so I elected to walk up the stairs, which were unfinished and dirty. As I climbed my heart sank, but on entering the offices of the legal firm all was as it should be, a hive of activity in reasonable office-like decor. To descend I took the lift which though speedy was stiflingly hot and once again found myself on the over-crowded pavement. Having signalled the driver we set off for the next appointment, but by now I was in air-conditioned seclusion looking out on the multitudes – a spectacle through the window glass. The driver enthusiastically started to tell me about the cricket and how the first Test against the Australians would soon be taking place – cricket is now also a religion in India. We passed by the Eden Gardens where the game would be played and I thought of the funeral a few months previous of Mother Teresa that had taken place in the same arena, the little old woman now an icon for poor and suffering and the icons of the sports fraternity, heroes of bat and ball capable of providing national pride or collective sorrow. When the traffic light created a pause the sellers of strawberries harassed me through the window and I observed a weary rickshaw *wallah* mopping his brow. Somehow everything and everyone had a bit part in an endless drama, and one minute I felt part of it and in the next was merely an observer.

The birthday party on our first visit was a thoroughly happy affair with lots of little people all intent on stuffing their mouths with crisps and sweeties; the *kooi* bag strung up on the ceiling was burst and the eager recipients of its little gifts scrambled about the floor picking things up as fast as possible. I recalled my own similar birthdays and the trouble my parents took to make them happy occasions. It was ever thus for the lucky ones. I did the same for my sons in their boyhood, agonising about what shape of birthday cake to devise and inventing games to play and win. At the end of such a day it is always special to see children content, tired and happy, playing with new toys and browsing through books. At Srila and Gopal's it was the same. The little girls helped their father make a list of all the toys that had been received so their donors could be thanked. In making the list each item was inspected and commented upon, but the older girl was quietly curled up already deeply absorbed by a new story. I resolved that in future my gifts would be books.

West Bengal was a very prosperous state and flourished under the British rule. This gave rise in turn to a flowering of culture, and the Bengali language was enriched by poets and writers such as Rabindranath Tagore. Temple building flourished and philosophers appeared – like Ramakrishna and Vivekananda. The British were not however the only colonisers. At Serampore the Danish East India company had carried on trade from the 17th century till 1845 when they sold their possessions to the British. Subsequently the Serampore College was established and incorporated in 1827 as a university by Danish Royal Charter. This was the first modern university in the whole of Asia. The College is still active and is now a Baptist theological institute.

At Chandernagore there is a gate bearing the motto of the French Republic: 'Liberte, Egalite Fraternite', and there had been an establishment of learning since 1673 to 1952. Even now though hardly anybody speaks French there is a French atmosphere with a church that resembles a French village church called the Église du Sacré Coeur along with its statue of Joan of Arc and a Lourdes grotto. My paternal grandmother Aline had family ties here; her father had been an indigo farmer and when they were orphaned the de Veria sisters grew up in Raja Santosh Road in Alipore, a fashionable suburb of Calcutta, where later I was to live as a small child.

The Dutch settled at Chinsura further north and ceded it to Britain in 1826 and there still remain a Dutch barracks, a church and a cemetery. The Armenians built St John's at Chinsura in 1695 and annually in January the Armenians from Calcutta come to hold joint services on St John's day. The Portuguese created the Church of Our Lady of Bandel in 1599 and it was rebuilt after being destroyed by Shah Jahan in 1632. The Portuguese controlled the majority of the trade that passed through West Bengal in the time of the Moghul Empire before the other European nations arrived. Bandel is still the site of an annual pilgrimage and also famous for the local little cheeses that are made there, I was so glad to be able to taste them again when staying with the Basus. At Imambara there is a Shiite mosque and further north of Hooghly are numerous Hindu temples of renown. The surrounding hundred miles around

Calcutta have a wealth of holy places to visit and absorb but getting around is challenging and only the most dedicated traveller would probably persevere.

CHAPTER FOURTEEN

A Fond Farewell 'Phir Milengi!'

In March I flew on to Mumbai, and Graham and I returned there in May on business. This is an unlovely city and though generally acknowledged to be India's most energetic and successful metropolis, home to the Indian Stock Exchange and centre for a huge film industry that rivals Hollywood in sheer output, I do not enjoy it as a place. By comparison to the other metropolitan cities it is expensive and full of a brashness with no real architectural charm. Arriving in daylight by air fills one with dismay – the shanty towns seem to stretch for miles. The hotels are all very expensive and the fact that it is a favourite leisure venue for the wealthy from the Middle Eastern kingdoms gives it a raffishness that I do not like. Indian society however is full of energy and the hospitality is as generous as ever and indeed we were warmly welcomed on three different occasions.

Travelling by car in Mumbai can take a long time. The city is spread along the coast and a car journey for dinner can easily take up to an hour or more one way. We count ourselves fortunate in having good friends and acquaintances in Mumbai but it will never be a favourite destination, more a base from which to visit Gujarat, Goa and the charming south of India.

The heat and humidity in May was quite simply overwhelming. The dry heat of Rajasthan or Delhi is infinitely preferable to this. As we finally left on a hot sticky night in May I reflected on a year that had seen me travel 50,000 miles on three occasions to and within India. Exhausted but happy I wondered when I would return, but determined to do so.

Beloved Bharat, land of my birth, there is so much yet to explore and experience: fishing on the Cauvery river for Mahseer in South India, Kerala and its many attractions, Sikkim for its famous flora, Himachal Pradesh for its lush valleys, a return to the source of the Ganges which I have not seen for nearly forty years, the wildlife parks and the great temples of South India, Gujarat and its ancient architecture, a truly marvellous choice, and always with the opportunity to meet up with or make good friends.

Sitting in my study, looking out on the green Peeblesshire hills covered in a light dusting of snow, with the sheep grazing contentedly, I look down and see a grey squirrel on the garden wall with two robins fighting for supremacy on the bird table. Raju my little black cat stretches and that action somehow reminds me of an Indian garden, with the shy movements of a mongoose venturing out in the morning sunshine. A blackbird enters the bird table impasse but in my mind's eye they are green parakeets and that screeching sound? Surely, that was the call of the peacock.

Aline Dobbie
Rosewood

Epilogue

Since I completed the book in January 1999 so much has happened personally to us as a family and to the world in general. Now that the book is to be published shortly I thought it appropriate to conclude with my current thinking that is relevant to India.

In the run up to Christmas 2001 to which we are greatly looking forward, as it will be the first time that our family will all be together after several years and with the addition of our first grandchild, I have been sorting out our book shelves, redistributing the titles and making way for the books we have either received or bought throughout the last year or two. There, in a top corner I found *Malakand Field Force 1897* by W. Spencer Churchill. Ours is a Colonial Silver Library Edition printed in 1901. A century later our televisions have been featuring the 21st-century's war in Afghanistan, yet reading Winston Churchill writing over a hundred years ago and looking at the detailed maps I am forced to murmur '... same country, different protagonists ...'

My thoughts have gone back to December 40 years ago when still a schoolgirl, singing carols in an old people's home in Winchester along with my peer group. After a rousing session we sat down and talked with the old folk. I had the good fortune to meet a very old gentleman who told me proudly he had fought in the Second Afghan War and he reminisced gently about it. He was thus prompted because I said I would be flying out to India for a family Christmas. I wish I had had the wit to write down what he said but I do remember him talking about harsh terrain, fear, cruelty and barbarism. Yes, indeed those are words with which we have all become very familiar in the last three months of this year.

Now, tragically, as I am writing, the news bulletins give details of a terrorist attack on the Indian Parliament. This could once more bring India and Pakistan to the edge of the abyss. I pray that both countries will behave with restraint and maturity.

Someone once wisely wrote that this quarrel is like a family feud between cousins. It could be said that Pakistan is perhaps the 'cousin' with the negative/poor relation attitude. India has a powerful idea of its own identity, and is a major force in South Asia, with armed forces totalling 1.26 million, and justifiably proud of its huge enduring democracy. Hopefully, diplomacy and a commitment to peace and a desire for co-existence will prevail.

In the decades to come when historians reflect on the twentieth century I think they will categorise it as 'a hundred years war'. This hundred years war will have been different from the medieval one, which only encompassed Europe; this one encompassed the world. Curiously though, if you talk to young people about the events and people of the twentieth century, among the great leaders and makers of history one man transcends all the others. Why? Because he wanted to change things peacefully. Gandhi's legacy to India is immeasurable and is an example to all of us.

For me it was a very emotional experience to visit Raj Ghat in Delhi and visit the site of Gandhiji's funeral pyre. I most sincerely recommend it as an essential visit to the traveller who visits Delhi. Having driven through the hustle and bustle of the city, when one finally arrives, takes off footwear and walks into the peaceful oasis that is Raj Ghat, there is a serenity and air of friendliness that exemplifies the dichotomy of India. Chaos, confusion, noise and perhaps even aggression on the roads and then silence, bird-song, a gentle smiling greeting from fellow Indian visitors. Sit awhile and look around and read the inscriptions. I found it comforting to purchase a small posy of flowers to lay on the plinth as others do. Watch the *mali* mowing the lawn, in the most timeless way – directing a bullock that is pulling a lawnmower – what could be more Indian or more engaging?

Gandhiji said that if we all did a little then a lot would be achieved. That is not a direct quotation but a distillation of his thoughts but it is timeless advice. Those of us who have connections with India or just visit can all do a little, or if circumstances allow, much more. The opportunities for practical help are many and varied. When natural disasters strike the United Kingdom is so generous and prompt in its giving, but on a regular basis there are significant ways to help, be it old people under Help the Aged's Adopt a Granny scheme, which I know to be very worthwhile and rewarding, or whole families picking up their lives after a disaster who can be sponsored through Christian Aid, or most important of all, helping to educate children. A happy childhood is the foundation of life but for a huge number of disadvantaged children just survival is their aim.

Westerners abhor the idea of child labour but in truth it is a reality for the poor in India. Despite legislation it is known that in the remote villages and rural areas 80 per cent of children between the ages of six and fourteen are in regular work and do not attend school. Similarly, children you as visitors might see on the streets of the big cities are eking a living, often without support from family, and yearn to have the opportunity for schooling.

My gentle suggestion is that if you have the good fortune to go and travel around India, perhaps in some style and comfort, and if you buy a lovely carpet or dhurries, think about helping to educate the young folk who very probably wove your new prized possession. Project Mala is just such an action programme for the scheduled castes and tribes, and their students between the ages of nine and eleven have never had the opportunity of formal education. Moreover, Project Mala does not discriminate between boys and girls and the student ratio is approximately fifty-fifty. The great sadness of child labour is that mostly these children grow up illiterate and miss out on their formative years, which has a lasting effect on their personal development. That in turn impacts on the country as a whole. Those of us who may have the opportunity to make a difference can find it infinitely rewarding.

It is estimated that there are over 250 million children deprived of their childhood worldwide, and Asia contributes to sixty per cent of this problem; within India alone there are approximately sixty million child labourers. The garment industry and several other like the diamond and gemstone cutting and polishing units and the manufacture of fireworks and matches, slates and pencils, glass and bangle works and other traditional manufacturers have historically employed young children. Affluent Indians are also known to employ young children as servants, much as was done in the United Kingdom in the nineteenth century and before. I would like to emphasise that what we Westerners now see as an abomination, we in this country and the rest of Europe have been guilty of in past centuries. Economic prosperity and education will be the dynamic to change this, but pragmatically it will take at least another fifty years to effect. SACCS (South Asian Coalition on Child Servitude) is another very worthwhile venture started in 1989. One of its most successful achievements is the establishment of the Mukti Ashram in New Delhi, which is a rehabilitation centre for freed child bonded labourers.

Another worthy cause is the Butterflies Programme for School and Working Children which is also in New Delhi and struggles heroically to help its young members to be educated and have some stability and security in their dangerous street lives.

India's five-star hotels are becoming increasingly famous for their 'out of this world' provision for well to do travellers. So many have come into being recently that it would be invidious to recommend any one, but I know personally that they provide unique friendly luxury and wonderful experiences. The Heritage Hotels have continued to expand and upgrade and I am continually sent fresh details on the delights that await us on another visit. Indeed Graham and I plan two visits – one will be to Kerala as we promised ourselves earlier, and the other is to the wildlife and game sanctuaries. Jungle odysseys are readily available at Kaziranga in Assam, or Corbett in the Himalayas, Ranthambore in Rajasthan, or Kanha in Central India and beckon with the promise of wonderful wildlife and that essential feeling of wilderness and timelessness. In the south there is Periyar, which can easily be included in a visit to Kerala.

Last year we travelled 32,000 miles on a tour of Malaysia, both peninsula and Borneo, Singapore, Brunei and Viet Nam. It was a very special and enjoyable trip, which I would thoroughly recommend to active and healthy people. Viet Nam is welcoming and interesting but relatively inexperienced in its tourist industry but they will catch up with the rest of the East very quickly. Malaysia offers both sophistication and primitive experiences to the traveller. However, on reflection I feel that India will always provide a wider choice of antiquity, history, colour, wildlife, beaches, trekking and that intangible quality of spiritual adventure – and perhaps spiritual fulfilment. On a more prosaic note, the variety of shopping is huge and intoxicating.

Finally I would say that those still left with a perception that India is a third world country with a crumbling transport system and people living in poverty please consider that this is the world's largest democracy of a billion people and the middle classes in India are equivalent to the whole population of the United States. Doctors, scientists and computer experts, accountants and management consultants from India are in demand all over the world. Materials originating in India influence the clothing industry worldwide and much of what we wear in the West is manufactured in the subcontinent.

The dichotomy of designer hotels in Delhi or the beach shack restaurants in Goa or Kerala, mist lifting from the lakes at Bharatpur revealing teeming wildlife, the cough of a tiger at Corbett in the undergrowth filling one with excitement and anticipation, watching the sunrise on the mountain peaks in the Himalayan range, diving off the Lakshadweep islands, it is all there for you to experience within the constraints of your own personal health, energy and vigour. However sophisticated and efficient the tourist industry might become in India it is possible to take a side step and experience this vast country's timeless rhythm and fundamental beauty.

I leave you with my abiding memory of a sunset and the peacocks preparing to roost for the night; the dark silhouettes of the birds in the trees with behind them the crimson glow of the sun setting and slowly descending with the sky gradually becoming deep blue and then black, and tomorrow bringing the promise of a new beautiful day.

December 2001

Useful Addresses

Children's Charities Mentioned in the Epilogue:

Project Mala: Town Farmhouse, 25 Church Lane, Nether Poppleton, York YO26 6LF. *Telephone:* 01904 786880 *Fax:* 01904 786881 email: info@projectmala.org. *Website:* www.projectmala.org. Reg No. 801953. *Patrons:* Felicity Kendal, Sir Mark Tully, Lady Young, The Maharajah of Benares India Office: Sarraf Kunj, Jangi Road, Mirzapur 231001 UP India. *email:* davidrangpal@satyam.net.in

Butterflies Programme of Street and Working Children: U-4 First Floor, Green Park Extension, New Delhi 110 016 India *email:* butterflieskids@sify.com

SACCS and Mukti Ashram: *Mukti Ashram:* Ibrahimpur, Burari-Mukhmelpur Road, Delhi 36 India, *SACCS:* L–6 Kalkajee, New Delhi, India. email: muktisaccs@yahoo.com

Wildlife Charity

LifeForce Charitable Trust, 1A High Street, Sherington, Newport Pagnell MK16 9NA. Telephone: 01908 211567. *Website:* www.lifeforceindia.com

Tourism

India Tourist Office: 7 Cork Street, London, W1X 3LH. Telephone: Brochure line 01233 211999. *Website:* www.indiatouristoffice.org. *email:* info@indiatouristoffice.org **Indus Tours & Travel Limited:** *MWB Business Exchange,* 2 Gayton Road, Harrow, Middlesex HA1 2XU. Telephone: 0208 901 7320. Fax: 0208 901 7321. *email:* indus@btinternet.com. *Website:* www. indus@industours.co.uk

For those interested in visiting Scotland's beautiful Scottish Borders: **The Scottish Borders:** *Website:* www.scot-borders.co.uk

Bibliography

Roberts, Field-Marshal Lord, of Kandahar VC GCB GCSI GCIE, 1897, *Forty-one Years in India*, London, Richard Bentley and Son

Beach, Milo Cleveland & Ebba Koch, and Wheeler Thackston, 1997, *The Padshanama King of the World*, a Moghul Manuscript from The Royal Library, Windsor Castle

Sunity Devee, Maharani of Cooch Behar & Rose, Aline, 1916, *Bengal Dacoits and Tigers*, Calcutta, Thacker Spink & Co.

Rose, Frank D, Lt Col., 1947, *A Brief Note on the Origin and History of the Jats and the Jat Regiment*, privately published

Mayo, Katherine, 1935, *The Face of Mother India*, London, Hamish Hamilton

Woodruff (Mason) Philip, 1953, *The Men Who Ruled India*, London, Jonathan Cape Ltd.

Mason, Philip, 1974, *A Matter of Honour – an account of the Indian Army, its Officers and Men*, London, Jonathan Cape Ltd.

Miller, Charles, 1977, *Khyber – The Story of the North West Frontier*, London, Macdonald & Jane's Publishers Ltd.

Tillotson, G H R, 1990, *Moghul India*, London, Penguin Books Ltd.

McCann, Charles, (n.d.), *Trees of India*, Bombay, D B Taraporevala Sons & Co.

'Silver Hackle', 1928, *Man-Eaters and other Denizens of the Indian Jungle*, Calcutta, Thacker Spink & Co.

Bainbridge Fletcher, T, 1936, *Birds of an Indian Garden*, Calcutta, Thacker Spink & Co.

Ali Salim, 1941, *The Book of Indian Birds*, Bombay, The Bombay Natural History Society